# WHAT THINGS ARE

# WHAT THINGS ARE

## A QUESTION-AND-ANSWER BOOK ABOUT OURSELVES AND OUR WORLD

**General Editor    Lesley Firth**

**KINGFISHER BOOKS**

Kingfisher Books, Grisewood & Dempsey Ltd,
Elsley House, 24–30 Great Titchfield Street,
London W1P 7AD

This revised edition published in 1990 by Kingfisher Books

Originally published in hardcover in 1984 as
*Question and Answer Encyclopedia: What Is It?*

Reprinted 1990

BRITISH LIBRARY CATALOGUING IN PUBLICATION DATA
What is it? What things are.
1. General knowledge – Questions & answers – For children
I. Firth, Lesley
793.73
ISBN 0 86272 400 7

Phototypeset by Southern Positives and Negatives (SPAN),
Lingfield, Surrey

Colour separations by Newsele Litho Ltd, Milan, Italy

Printed in Spain by Artes Gráficas Toledo, S.A.
D.L.TO:723-1990

**Authors**
Neil Ardley
David Lambert
Mark Lambert
James Muirden
Brian Williams
Jill Wright

**Artists**
Bob Bampton/The Garden Studio
Norma Burgin/John Martin & Artists
Dave Etchell & John Ridyard
Oliver Frey/Temple Art Agency
Rob Jobson/Tudor Art Studios
Charlotte Kennedy
Bernard Robinson/Tudor Art Studios
Mike Roffe
Chris Ryley/John Martin & Artists
Mike Saunders/Jillian Burgess
Tammy Wong/John Martin & Artists

# CONTENTS

## OURSELVES

## TRANSPORT

## SCIENCE

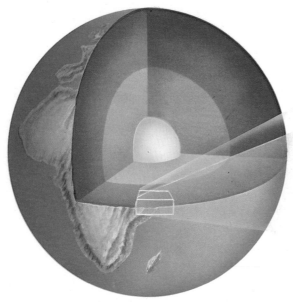

## THE PAST

## HOW PEOPLE LIVE

## ARTS AND SPORT

## INDEX

# PLANTS AND ANIMALS

▼ WHAT MAKES LIVING
THINGS GROW?

**All living things grow by
increasing the number of
their cells. Cells grow to
their full size and then
divide.**

When a cell divides, everything in it divides. Most importantly, the nucleus divides
and each chromosome is
duplicated.

Usually, the chromosomes
of a cell are not visible. But as
the cell begins to divide, its
chromosomes appear as long,
thin threads in the nucleus
(1). Then the chromosomes
begin to shorten (2). As they
do so, they split into two
chromatids, which remain
joined at one point (3). Meanwhile, a cell organelle known
as the centrosome divides and
begins to form a spindle outside the nucleus.

At this stage, the outer
membrane of the nucleus
breaks down. The chromosomes are lined up on a
central 'plate' and become
attached to the threads of the
spindle (4). Then the
chromatids separate (5) and
move towards opposite ends
of the cell (6). Two new
nuclear membranes form and
the rest of the cell divides (7).

▶ WHAT IS A CELL?

**Cells are the basic building blocks of living things.
Each one is made up of a
membrane surrounding a
small quantity of jelly-like
material called protoplasm.**

All living things are made
from cells. Some plants and
animals have only one cell,
but many more are made up
of millions of cells.

Each cell is like a tiny
factory. It contains all the
chemicals and structures it
needs to play its part in the
animal or plant to which it
belongs.

The cell protoplasm
consists of the nucleus and the
cytoplasm. The nucleus is the
central controller of the cell.
It contains complicated
chemicals called DNA
(deoxyribonucleic acid) and
RNA (ribonucleic acid). The
nucleus uses these substances
to send out a stream of
chemical instructions to other
structures that lie in the
cytoplasm.

The cell is held inside a thin
membrane called the plasma
membrane. Water and
chemicals can pass through
this membrane, so neighbouring cells are able to
transfer substances from one
to another.

In animals, the plasma
membrane is all that surrounds a cell. But plants have
an extra, much thicker cell
wall, made of a fibrous
material called cellulose.

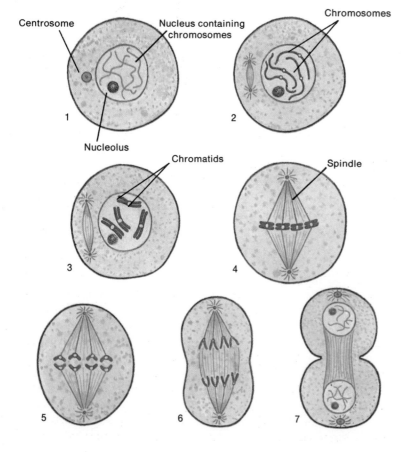

Centrosome
Nucleus containing chromosomes
Chromosomes
Nucleolus
1
2
Chromatids
Spindle
3
4
5
6
7

10

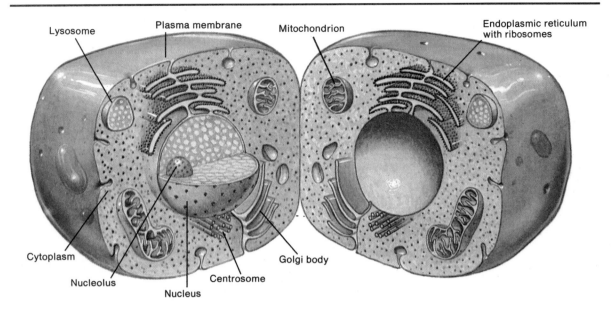

Lysosome · Plasma membrane · Mitochondrion · Endoplasmic reticulum with ribosomes · Cytoplasm · Nucleolus · Nucleus · Centrosome · Golgi body

## ▲ WHAT ARE CELL ORGANELLES?

**The tiny structures floating in the watery cytoplasm of a cell are known as organelles. They do the work of the cell 'factory'.**

Cells need energy to do their work, and this is supplied by tiny, sausage-like bodies called mitochondria. These are the 'power houses' of the cell factory.

Another very important cell structure is the system of channels called the endo-plasmic reticulum. The channels are held inside mem-branes, and tiny round bodies called ribosomes lie on the membranes. The system makes proteins, and it also helps to carry materials from one part of the cell to another.

Other cell organelles include chloroplasts (in plants) and the bean-shaped lysosomes. The lysosomes contain enzymes for dealing with bacteria and damaged cell material. The golgi body, a system of bag-like channels, helps to remove waste materials from the cell.

## ▲ WHAT ARE CHROMO-SOMES AND GENES?

**The chromosomes of a cell are long, thread-like bodies inside the nucleus. They contain the chemical DNA and are made up of long chains of units called genes. Each gene controls a particular feature of the animal or plant.**

Chromosomes are mostly made up of DNA. This chemical is unique because it can make copies of itself. When a chromosome divides, each chromatid contains DNA that is identical in every way to the DNA in the original chromosome.

Every feature of a plant or animal is controlled by the DNA in one or more short lengths of chromosome inside the cell. Each of these lengths is called a gene. In humans, for example, there are genes that control eye colour.

Each species of animal and plant has its own set of chromosomes with its own set of genes. And because DNA can make copies of itself, genes can be passed from one generation to the next.

## ▲ HOW DOES FOOD BECOME ENERGY?

**Food sugars are broken down in a series of chemical changes. Oxygen is used up in this process and carbon dioxide, water and energy are produced.**

The process of making energy from food is called respir-ation. It involves a long series of chemical reactions. The starting point of the process is the sugar glucose.

The first stages of glucose breakdown take place in the cytoplasm and do not need oxygen. The later stages can only occur when there is oxygen present. They take place inside the cell's mito-chondria. Here, the energy contained in the original glucose is used to create high-energy molecules of a substance called ATP.

The energy in ATP can then be used for powering muscle movement, building up proteins and other body processes. As ATP is created, the chemical reactions that occur in the mitochondria produce water and carbon dioxide as waste products.

### ▼ WHAT ARE VIRUSES AND BACTERIA?

**Viruses and bacteria are the smallest living things. Viruses have no cell walls and can only work properly inside the cells of other living organisms. Bacteria are larger than viruses and can exist by themselves.**

A virus is made up of a protein coat wrapped around a small amount of DNA or RNA. It can reproduce itself but only when it is inside a

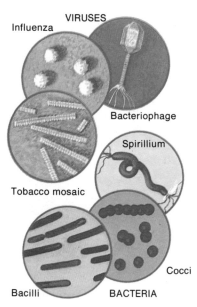

VIRUSES
Influenza
Bacteriophage
Tobacco mosaic
Spirillium
Bacilli
Cocci
BACTERIA

living cell. Viruses are therefore on the borderline between living and non-living things. When they invade cells they usually cause disease.

Bacteria are tiny, single-celled organisms. Some are round, others are rod-shaped and some even look like cork-screws.

Some bacteria cause disease but many others are useful. A large number feed by breaking down dead plant and animal matter. They release chemicals into the soil that can be used by plants.

### ▼ WHAT IS A PLANT?

**A living thing that makes its own food by photosynthesis is called a plant. Nearly all plants have cellulose cell walls.**

Like all living things, plants feed, grow, breathe (respiration) and get rid of waste materials. They can also make certain movements and are sensitive to certain stimuli.

But what sets plants apart from animals is the fact that they make their own food by photosynthesis. For this they need the green pigment chlorophyll, which is why most plants are green.

There are, of course, some exceptions to this rule. Parasitic plants, such as dodder and broomrape, do not contain chlorophyll, but they have cellulose cell walls like normal plants.

Fungi, on the other hand, are not like other plants. In fact, they are sometimes placed in a separate group called the Protista, together with the bacteria and all single-celled living things.

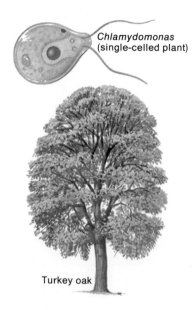

*Chlamydomonas* (single-celled plant)

Turkey oak

### ▼ WHAT IS AN ANIMAL?

**An animal is a living thing that feeds by taking in organic matter. Its cell walls are usually non-rigid. Most animals can move about and have nervous systems.**

An animal cannot make its own food. It has to feed on material obtained from plants or other animals.

In other ways animals are similar to plants. They grow, reproduce, breathe and get rid of waste matter. However, to

Sea anemone

Mink

obtain food, animals have to be able to reach it or draw it towards them in some way. So animals must be able to move, and animals that perform complicated movements have nervous systems to control their bodies.

It is sometimes difficult to tell the difference between an animal and a plant. For example, the single-celled organism *Euglena* has chloroplasts and is often classed as a plant. However, it can also feed in an animal-like way. So some biologists classify *Euglena* as an animal.

## ▼ WHAT IS EVOLUTION?

**Evolution is the process of slow change that takes place in populations of animals and plants.**

Very few species of animals and plants remain the same over a long period of time. Each generation may have features that are different from those of the generation before. These changes may lead to new species being formed.

Evolution has been responsible for the appearance of all modern living things. From the study of fossils, and other work, it is possible to see how some groups have evolved.

The first vertebrates (animals with backbones) to appear, about 500 million years ago, were fishes. Many groups of fishes appeared in the seas over the next 100 million years. Gradually some fishes left the water and developed as amphibians. In turn, some of these land animals evolved into reptiles, the group from which birds and mammals arose.

## ▼ WHAT IS NATURAL SELECTION?

**Evolution has taken place over many years because of natural selection. Animals and plants that are suited to their surroundings survive. Those that cannot compete die out.**

Sometimes an animal or plant accidentally develops a new characteristic. This may make it more (or less) able to survive than one that has not developed such a feature.

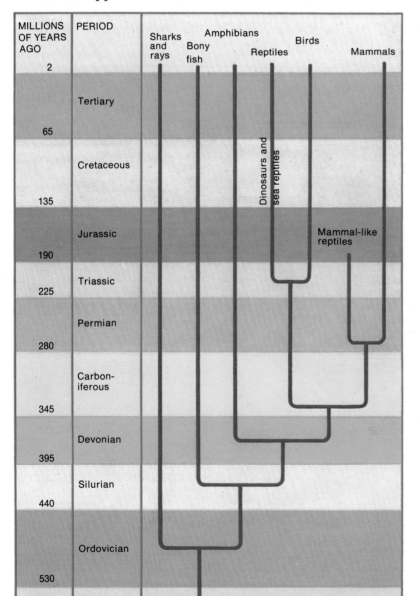

| MILLIONS OF YEARS AGO | PERIOD | Sharks and rays | Bony fish | Amphibians | Reptiles | Dinosaurs and sea reptiles | Birds | Mammal-like reptiles | Mammals |
|---|---|---|---|---|---|---|---|---|---|
| 2 | | | | | | | | | |
| | Tertiary | | | | | | | | |
| 65 | | | | | | | | | |
| | Cretaceous | | | | | | | | |
| 135 | | | | | | | | | |
| | Jurassic | | | | | | | | |
| 190 | | | | | | | | | |
| | Triassic | | | | | | | | |
| 225 | | | | | | | | | |
| | Permian | | | | | | | | |
| 280 | | | | | | | | | |
| | Carbon-iferous | | | | | | | | |
| 345 | | | | | | | | | |
| | Devonian | | | | | | | | |
| 395 | | | | | | | | | |
| | Silurian | | | | | | | | |
| 440 | | | | | | | | | |
| | Ordovician | | | | | | | | |
| 530 | | | | | | | | | |

PEPPERED MOTHS

Light, speckled form

Dark form

Peppered moths show natural selection in action today. There are two varieties of this moth, one light-coloured type and a dark type.

Before the Industrial Revolution in Great Britain, the dark moths were rare. They were easily spotted by birds as they rested on the lichen-covered bark of trees. But pollution began to kill the lichen and blacken the trees. So the dark moths became the ones that were well camouflaged and the light-coloured moths soon began to decrease in numbers.

13

## ▼ WHAT ARE SINGLE-CELLED PLANTS?

**Single-celled plants belong to the large group known as the algae. There are many different forms. Some can move about using whip-like flagella.**

The algae are the world's simplest plants. They have no roots, stems or leaves and a large number consist of just one cell. Such plants often float freely in lakes and oceans. They form, together with tiny animals, a drifting mass called plankton.

Like other plants, algae contain chlorophyll. Many algae are therefore green, but in some the colour is hidden by other pigments.

Single-celled green algae include forms such as *Pleurococcus*, which can be found on the moist bark of trees, and pond algae such as *Euglena* and *Chlamydomonas*. Other single-celled algae include the yellow-green algae, golden algae and dinoflagellates.

Diatoms, such as *Coscinodiscus*, form the largest group. They have cell walls made of silica.

## ▼ WHAT ARE SEAWEEDS?

**Seaweeds also belong to the plant group called the algae. They are many-celled plants.**

The smallest many-celled algae include plants like the *Volvox*, which is a hollow ball of cells, and the pondweed *Spirogyra*. This consists of long strings, or filaments, of cells. The many-celled algae found in the sea are known as seaweeds.

Among the simplest green seaweeds is sea lettuce *(Ulva)*, which consists of a flat, two-layered 'leaf'. Its relative, *Enteromorpha*, has tube-like fronds. *Cladophora* is made up of long branched filaments or strands.

Brown seaweeds include the familiar wracks *(Fucus)* and kelps, or oarweeds *(Laminaria)*. Most of these are attached to rocks, but some float freely in the sea. The Sargasso Sea is named after its vast floating rafts of *Sargassum* seaweed.

Red seaweeds are usually smaller and many have complicated structures. Most live in deep water.

Scots pine    Spruce

Cedar

Larch    Cypress

## ▲ WHAT ARE CONIFERS?

**Conifers are seed-bearing plants. But unlike flowering plants, they produce seeds in cones.**

Conifers are easy to recognize. They all have leathery, needle-like or scale-like leaves and they produce cones.

Conifers include the pines, spruces, firs, larches, hemlocks, cedars, cypresses and junipers.

All these species, except the larches and the swamp cypress, are evergreen. This means that they bear leaves at all times of the year. They are able to do this because their tough leaves conserve water and do not need to be shed when water is scarce. They can also withstand wind and frost.

In fact, evergreen conifers do shed their leaves. But leaves are being grown and shed all the time. Each leaf lives for about three years.

Because conifers can stand up to harsh conditions, they can grow in places where broadleaved trees cannot. Most grow in a broad band just below the Arctic Circle.

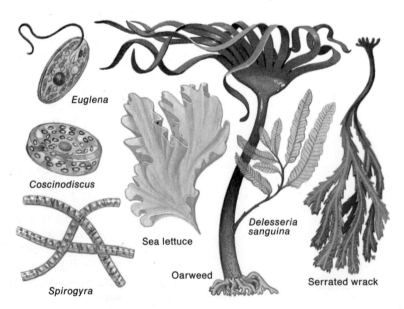

Euglena

Coscinodiscus

Spirogyra

Sea lettuce

Oarweed

*Delesseria sanguina*

Serrated wrack

## ▼ WHAT ARE MOSSES?

**Mosses are low-growing plants that have no true roots. Together with the liverworts, they form the plant group known as Bryophytes.**

Mosses form mats or small cushions in several different places. They grow on the ground in woodlands, on the bark of trees, on moist banks, in bogs and on rocks. In fact, they grow in places where flowering plants find it difficult to grow.

A moss plant has a thin stem with a number of simple leaves attached. The plant has no roots but holds onto the ground using root-like threads called rhizoids. Most moss plants can conduct water up their stems. They reproduce by means of spores which develop in capsules.

The largest European moss is the hair moss (*Polytrichum commune*). In damp places its stems can reach a height of 20 centimetres. The water moss (*Fontinalis antipyretica*) lives in streams and ponds. Its long straggling stems may be over 100 centimetres long.

## ▼ WHAT IS A LIVERWORT?

**Liverworts belong to the same plant group as mosses. Some have simple, flat plant bodies, others are more like mosses.**

Liverworts dry out more easily than mosses and so are only found in damp, shady places. Those with flat plant bodies are known as thalloid liverworts. They have no stems or true leaves and they sprawl across the wet ground, clinging on with tiny rhizoids. Thalloid liverworts include such types as *Pellia*.

Over 90 per cent of liverworts are of the moss-like type, known as leafy liverworts. They have stems and thin, filmy leaves. *Lophocolea* grows on bark in dark woods.

Like mosses, liverworts reproduce by means of spores that develop inside capsules. But the liverwort capsules develop more slowly.

Most liverworts can also reproduce in another way. They grow small round or disc-shaped structures on their leaves. Each one can become a new plant.

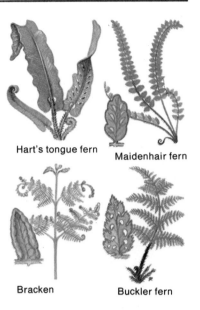

Hart's tongue fern

Maidenhair fern

Bracken

Buckler fern

## ▲ WHAT ARE FERNS?

**Ferns are another group of plants that make spores. But, unlike mosses and liverworts, they can live in fairly dry places.**

Ferns range from smallish plants that grow in the world's temperate regions to tall, tropical tree ferns.

They are much larger than mosses for two reasons. First, their stems contain good water-conducting cells for carrying water up to their leaves. Second, adult ferns produce only spores. Their sex cells, which need moisture, develop on tiny heart-shaped structures called prothalli. These develop from spores lying on the ground.

An adult fern is anchored to the ground by an underground stem, or rhizome. Above the ground there are one or more leaves, or fronds.

Sometimes the fronds have simple shapes, like the hart's tongue fern, which has strap-like leaves. But more often fronds are divided into leaflets known as pinnae. These may be divided into smaller leaflets called pinnules.

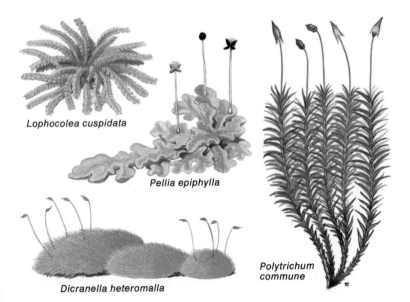

Lophocolea cuspidata

Pellia epiphylla

Dicranella heteromalla

Polytrichum commune

## ▶ WHAT ARE FLOWERING PLANTS?

**These are plants that produce their reproductive organs in flowers. This huge group of plants includes a wide range of herbaceous (green-stemmed) plants, shrubs and trees.**

Conifers and their relatives belong to the plant group known as gymnosperms. The word *gymnosperm* means 'naked seed' and these plants produce seeds that are exposed to the air.

Flowering plants, or angiosperms ('enclosed seed'), on the other hand, produce seeds that are surrounded by an ovary wall, which often develops into a fruit.

There are about 360,000 known species in the plant kingdom. Over 220,000 of these are flowering plants. They are very successful because of two important factors. First, their methods of seed formation and seed dispersal are very efficient. Second, they are a very adaptable group of plants. There are flowering plants in most of the world's environments, including deserts and high mountains.

There are two main groups of flowering plants. Monocotyledons are those with long, thin leaves with parallel veins. Their flowers almost always have three or six petals. This group includes grasses, bulb plants such as bluebells, and orchids. Only a few tropical monocotyledons, such as palm trees, are large.

Dicotyledons form a much bigger group. Their leaves are usually broad with a network of veins. Their flowers usually have four, five or many petals.

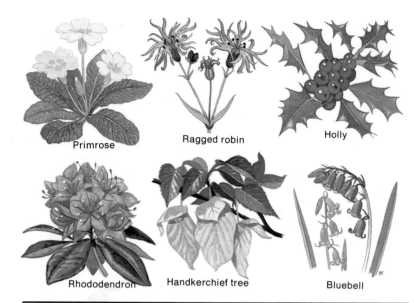

Primrose

Ragged robin

Holly

Rhododendron

Handkerchief tree

Bluebell

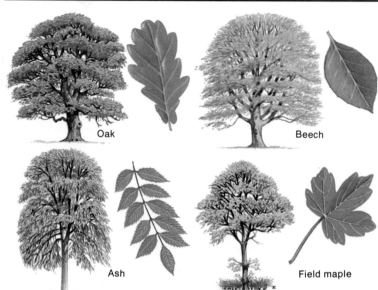

Oak

Beech

Ash

Field maple

## ▲ WHAT ARE DECIDUOUS TREES?

**Deciduous trees lose their leaves in autumn. They are mostly the broad-leaved trees of the northern hemisphere.**

Winter in the northern hemisphere is too harsh for most broadleaved trees. So they let their leaves fall in autumn and survive the winter in a state of dormancy (sleep). If they did not do this, their leaves would be damaged by wind and frost. And during severe frost they would lose more water than they could take up from the ground.

Deciduous, broadleaved woodlands are found in Europe, but North America and Eastern Asia have the greatest variety of trees. In North America there are about 100 different species, including maples, magnolias, hickories and tulip trees.

European deciduous woodlands have mostly oaks, ash, beech, birch or alder. Other European trees include hornbeam, whitebeam, field maple and mountain ash, or rowan.

## ▼ WHICH ARE THE LARGEST FLOWERING PLANTS?

**The world's largest plant is a Chinese wisteria.**

The Chinese wisteria at Sierra Madre in California has branches over 150 metres long. It produces about one and a half million flowers each year.

Another large plant is the giant Bolivian bromeliad *Puya raymondii*. Its spikes of 8000 flowers reach ten metres high.

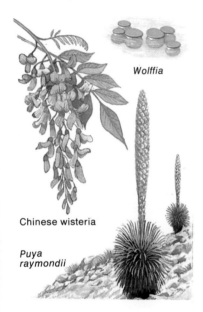

*Wolffia*

Chinese wisteria

*Puya raymondii*

## ▲ WHICH ARE THE SMALLEST FLOWERING PLANTS?

**The smallest flowering plant is the duckweed *Wolffia punctata*.**

Duckweeds form large floating masses on ponds. But each plant is tiny, consisting of one or more disc-like 'leaves' with a few hanging roots.

The smallest duckweeds belong to the genus *Wolffia*. *Wolffia* plants can measure just half a millimetre across.

## ▲ WHICH TREES GROW THE TALLEST?

**The world's tallest trees are found in the USA. They are the gigantic coast redwoods of California. But other trees also reach great heights.**

The tallest living coast redwood, known as 'Tallest Tree', is over 111 metres high. However, its top is dying and it probably once reached over 112 metres.

Other trees living in the same place have healthy tops and stand over 110 metres high. They may one day overtake 'Tallest Tree'.

Even taller trees may have existed in the past. A eucalyptus tree in Australia is believed to have reached 114 metres in 1880, and a Douglas fir felled in British Columbia in 1895 may have been over 127 metres high.

The world's largest trees are also found in California. They are the massive giant sequoias. The largest of these stands 85 metres high and measures over 24 metres round the trunk near its base.

## ▲ WHICH TREES LIVE THE LONGEST?

**The world's oldest trees are the bristlecone pines. Some are believed to be over 4500 years old.**

Until the early 1900s, scientists thought that the giant sequoias were the oldest living trees. Some of them have existed for 3400 years. But the bristlecone pines of the White Mountains in California are even older.

The oldest specimen of bristlecone pine that has been recorded was 4900 years old. It was cut down in 1969. The oldest living tree, called 'Methuselah', is believed to be 4600 years old.

Bristlecone pines live in a harsh environment, 3000 metres above sea level, on bare mountain slopes. There they grow into stunted, twisted forms.

Scientists have estimated that bristlecone pines could reach an age of 5500 years. But they also suggest that giant sequoias could live for 6000 years.

### ▼ WHAT ARE FUNGI?

**Fungi are thread-like organisms that reproduce by means of spores. Some fungi produce their spores in large fruiting bodies which we know as toadstools, brackets, cups, puffballs and jellies.**

Fungi are classed as plants, but their cell walls do not contain cellulose. Also, they do not contain the green pigment chlorophyll and cannot make their own food. They have to take their food from what is around them. Some fungi feed on dead and decaying plant or animal material.

Other fungi are parasites and take their food from living plants or animals.

The word 'fungus' usually makes us think of a toadstool. But the toadstool is only the fruiting body. The main part of the fungus is a mass of fungal threads called the mycelium. This is always hidden in the soil or wood on which the toadstool is growing.

Fungi that produce large fruiting bodies are the most advanced types. Apart from the familiar mushrooms and toadstools there are cup fungi, puffballs, jelly fungi and bracket fungi. Dry rot in houses is caused by a fungus with a large fruiting body.

But not all fungi produce large fruiting bodies. Simple fungi include moulds, mildews and parasites such as potato blight.

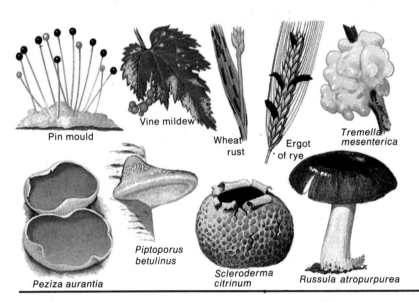

Pin mould

Vine mildew

Wheat rust

Ergot of rye

*Tremella mesenterica*

*Peziza aurantia*

*Piptoporus betulinus*

*Scleroderma citrinum*

*Russula atropurpurea*

### ▲ WHICH FUNGI ARE GOOD TO EAT?

**Field mushrooms are delicious and popular. But these are not the only kinds of fungi that are good to eat.**

Field mushroom

Parasol mushroom

Shaggy ink cap

Fairy ring champignon

Blusher

Cep

Giant puffball

Chanterelle

Oyster mushroom

Truffle

Morel

When field mushrooms appear in September and October, they are quite easy to recognize. But this is also true of several other kinds of edible mushrooms and toadstools.

In fields you may find giant puffballs which are delicious when cut into 'steaks' and fried. Fairy ring champignons have a nutty taste and shaggy ink caps, which cannot be mistaken for anything else, are also good.

In woods you may be lucky enough to come across other delicious fungi. Parasol mushrooms and bright yellow chanterelles are really worth searching for. Morels are a well-known delicacy in some places. Ceps are also popular, and blushers (which *must* be cooked) are even better. Oyster mushrooms can be found growing on trees.

Truffles are a great delicacy. They are not easy to find, as they grow underground in certain beechwoods.

*Never eat any toadstool that you cannot identify for certain.*

### ▼ WHICH TOADSTOOLS ARE POISONOUS?

**Poisonous toadstools must never be eaten. Many can cause extreme illness and some can cause death.**

Of all the toadstools, only a few are actually good to eat. Most are tasteless or even unpleasant. And some are poisonous and must be avoided at all costs.

The death cap and destroying angel are deadly poisonous. Eating either of these usually results in death.

Death cap

Panther cap

Destroying angel

Fly agaric

Devil's boletus

Yellow stainer

*Inocybe patouillardi*

Sickener
*Russula emetica*

The panther cap is only slightly less poisonous. Devil's boletus and the striking red and white fly agaric are also poisonous, but not usually fatal. Most species of *Inocybe* are poisonous and quite difficult to identify.

There are less harmful, but still poisonous toadstools. *Russula emetica* may cause sickness. The yellow stainer can be mistaken for a field mushroom, but its flesh stains yellow when bruised. People who eat this toadstool may develop alarming symptoms, but they always recover.

### ▼ WHICH FUNGI ARE USED IN FOOD-MAKING AND DRUGS?

**As well as edible fungi, there are others that are useful. *Penicillium* and other moulds produce antibiotic drugs, and yeasts are essential in making bread and alcoholic drinks.**

In 1929 Alexander Fleming noticed that *Penicillium* mould destroyed bacteria. Some years later, scientists took the antibacterial agent from *Penicillium* and called it penicillin. Since then, antibiotic drugs have been obtained from other moulds. *Penicillium* is also used in the making of certain cheeses.

Another important group of fungi are the yeasts, which can turn sugar into ethyl alcohol and carbon dioxide. They are used in the making of alcoholic drinks.

In bread-making, yeast produces carbon dioxide bubbles, which cause the dough to rise. When the bread is cooked, the yeast dies and the alcohol evaporates.

Yeast

Penicillium

### ▼ WHICH PLANTS ARE TWO PLANTS IN ONE?

**A lichen is not a single plant. It consists of a fungus and an alga tightly bound together. Both plants benefit from this arrangement.**

The outer layers of a lichen are made up of densely-packed fungal threads. These protect the inner layers. Nearer the centre the fungal threads are looser and surround the cells of an alga.

The alga obtains protection

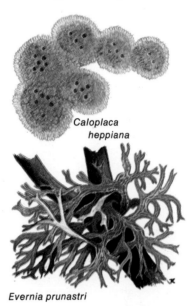

*Caloplaca heppiana*

*Evernia prunastri*

from wind, frost and sunlight. In return it supplies the fungus with food, which the alga makes by photosynthesis.

Some lichens encrust rocks, others have a leafy or shrubby appearance and can be found on trees. Lichens can reproduce themselves by producing a powdery mass of structures that contain pieces of both partners.

The fungus can also produce spores. When these are scattered, they form new lichens only if they come into contact with the right alga.

### ▼ WHAT ARE SINGLE-CELLED ANIMALS?

**Single-celled animals make up the group known as protozoans. They include amoebas, *Paramecium* and the malaria parasite.**

The most familiar single-celled animals are the amoebas. These are tiny, jelly-like animals that constantly change their shape. Relatives of the amoebas include the foraminiferans, which have shells, and radiolarians, which have delicate skeletons made of silica.

Some protozoans move about by using whip-like appendages called flagella. *Trypanosoma* is a flagellate that causes sleeping sickness in humans.

Other protozoans have tiny hairs known as cilia. *Paramecium* uses its cilia for swimming, while *Stentor* uses its cilia to create water currents which bring it food.

The last group of protozoans are all parasites. They include the malaria parasite *Plasmodium*.

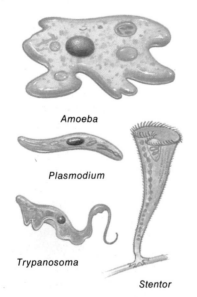

*Amoeba*

*Plasmodium*

*Trypanosoma*

*Stentor*

### ▼ WHAT ARE JELLYFISH?

**Jellyfish belong to the animal group known as coelenterates. This group also includes sea anemones and corals.**

A typical jellyfish is a large, umbrella-like 'bag' with tentacles hanging below it. The bag keeps the animal floating in the water while the tentacles catch food.

This is the adult stage of the jellyfish, known as the medusa stage. The eggs of most jellyfish do not develop

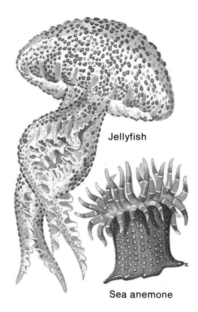

Jellyfish

Sea anemone

directly into medusae. Instead they develop first into polyps, which attach themselves to rocks or other surfaces. There they feed and grow before developing into medusae.

In other coelenterates the polyp is the adult stage and in sea anemones it is the only stage. They remain attached to rocks and their stinging tentacles seize prey.

The Portuguese man-o'-war may look like a jellyfish, but it is actually a floating colony of polyps suspended under a gas-filled bag.

### ▼ WHAT IS A CORAL?

**Corals are closely related to sea anemones. But sea anemones are usually large and unprotected, while corals are small and protect themselves with a chalky skeleton.**

The lumps of coral that can be bought in shops are only the skeletons of once-living animals. Living coral is really a skeleton covered with a fleshy mass of polyps, which are often brightly coloured.

A coral colony begins to form when a young polyp reproduces itself by budding. New polyps formed in this way also reproduce themselves, and so the colony grows.

The polyps remain connected to each other and they share the food caught by the colony. Each one produces its own part of the chalky skeleton.

Corals can be found in most seas, but the reef-forming types prefer warm, shallow water. A coral reef begins as a fringing reef along the shore of a continent or island.

HELIOPORA BLUE CORAL

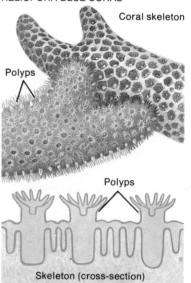

Coral skeleton

Polyps

Polyps

Skeleton (cross-section)

## ▼ WHAT ARE FLATWORMS?

**Flatworms are simple-bodied, flat, worm-like animals. Most are between one and ten millimetres long, but some tropical land species are much larger.**

Flatworms are found in most temperate and tropical regions of the world. Some live underneath stones and leaves in freshwater streams and ponds, but most live in the sea. Some tropical kinds are brightly coloured. A few flatworms live on land and some tropical land species measure over 30 centimetres.

Flatworms are famous for being able to regenerate, or remake, parts of their bodies. In fact, if a flatworm is cut up into several pieces, each piece will grow into a new flatworm. Some flatworms even reproduce naturally by tearing themselves in half! Flatworms are mostly free-living animals. However, some are parasites and their close relatives, which include the flukes and tapeworms, are all parasites.

Freshwater flatworm

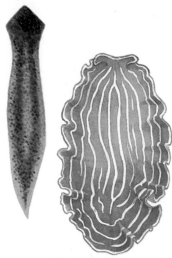

Tropical sea flatworm

## ▼ WHAT ARE MOLLUSCS?

**Molluscs are basically animals with shells. But some, such as squids, have internal shells. Others, such as slugs and octopuses, have no shells at all.**

Slugs and snails belong to the mollusc group known as gastropods. This is the largest mollusc group and also includes such animals as limpets, top shells, cowries, cone shells, brightly coloured sea slugs and sea butterflies.

The bivalves are another large group. Usually, all members of this group have a two-part shell, hinged in the middle. But different forms are adapted to different ways of life. Cockles are shallow sand burrowers, whereas sand gapers burrow deeper. Razor shells can burrow very rapidly. Mussels and oysters are attached to rocks. Scallops are swimming bivalves.

The largest molluscs are the cephalopods, such as squids, cuttlefish and octopuses.

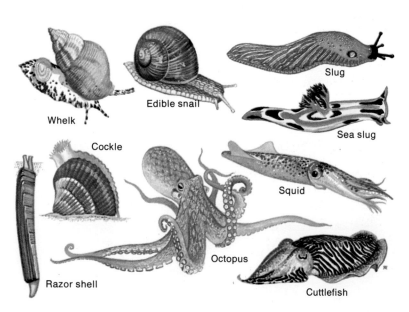

Whelk · Edible snail · Slug · Sea slug · Cockle · Razor shell · Squid · Octopus · Cuttlefish

## ▲ WHICH IS THE BIGGEST SQUID?

**The world's largest known squid is the Atlantic giant squid.**

In 1878 an Atlantic giant squid was washed up on the shores of Newfoundland in Canada. It weighed about two tonnes and its body measured 6.1 metres. Its tentacles measured another 10.65 metres, making a total length of 16.76 metres.

Giant squid are the world's largest invertebrates (animals without backbones). They feed on fish, crustaceans and smaller squid.

Giant squid probably spend most of their lives in deep water. But sometimes they may venture near the surface.

Brief sightings of these huge sea animals may have started off some of the legends about sea serpents and other monsters. According to Norse (Norwegian) legend, a *kraken* was supposed to be about two kilometres long! It was said to snatch crewmen from ships with its long tentacles.

Scorpion

Bird-eating spider

### ◀ WHAT ARE SPIDERS AND SCORPIONS?

**Spiders and scorpions belong to the group known as arachnids. They have hard outer skeletons like insects, but they have eight legs instead of six.**

The arachnids are a group that includes scorpions as well as ticks, mites and harvestmen (daddy-long-legs). But spiders are the most familiar of the arachnids.

The body of a spider is divided into two separate parts and its head bears a pair of poison fangs. Many spiders build webs for catching prey but others catch prey by simply chasing it. Trapdoor spiders lie in wait in specially constructed burrows.

A scorpion carries its poison in a sting at the end of its long curving tail. Instead of poison fangs the head bears a pair of large pincers for seizing prey.

Most scorpions use their sting to kill their prey before chewing it up with their pincers. Sometimes scorpions use their sting for defence.

### ▶ WHICH ANIMALS ARE CRUSTACEANS?

**The group known as crustaceans includes many kinds of many-legged, hard-bodied animals. The best-known of these are the lobsters, crabs, shrimps and wood-lice. Barnacles are also crustaceans.**

Crustaceans are different from other arthropods (animals with hard bodies and jointed legs). They have two antennae, or feelers. In addition, they have more legs than other arthropods and their legs are often two-branched. Many crustaceans have a carapace, or shell.

Most crustaceans are tiny, sea-dwelling animals, such as brine shrimps, ostracods and barnacles. However, water fleas live in fresh water and woodlice are land dwellers.

The largest crustaceans are known as decapods (ten legs). Shrimps and prawns are swimming crustaceans. Crabs and lobsters use their legs for walking and have large pincers.

Lobster

Crab

Prawn

Woodlouse

Barnacle

Water flea
*Daphnia*

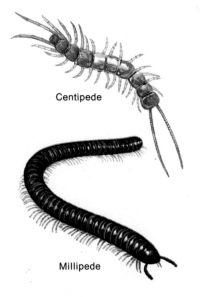

Centipede

Millipede

### ◀ WHAT IS THE DIFFERENCE BETWEEN CENTIPEDES AND MILLIPEDES?

**Centipedes and millipedes are both arthropods. But while centipedes are flesh-eaters, millipedes live on plant material.**

The name *centipede* means '100 legs' and the name *millipede* means '1000 legs'. But this is not always true. Some centipedes have as few as 30 legs and others have up to 340 legs. Millipedes usually do have more legs than centipedes, but no millipede has more than 400 legs and some have only 26 legs.

Centipedes are all fast-moving carnivores that feed on insects and other small animals. They have flattened, flexible bodies with one pair of legs on each segment.

Millipedes, on the other hand, are slow, plant-eating animals. Their bodies are usually round and the body segments are fused into double segments, each of which bears two pairs of legs.

## ▼ WHAT IS AN INSECT?

**Insects are hard-bodied animals with six legs. Their bodies are divided into three parts and many insects have wings.**

More than 85 per cent of the world's known animals are insects. About one million species have already been discovered and there may be another four million species we do not know about.

Like other arthropods, insects have hard outer skeletons and jointed legs. However, they are different from other arthropods in some ways. Their bodies are divided into three parts: head, thorax and abdomen. In addition, there are three pairs of legs on the thorax and often one or two pairs of wings.

Insects can be found in almost every habitat except the sea. Some primitive, wingless insects include springtails and bristletails.

Winged insects include dragonflies, grasshoppers, mantids, termites, bugs, moths, butterflies, true flies, ants, beetles and wasps.

## ▼ WHICH ARE THE LARGEST LIVING INSECTS?

**The world's largest insects include the fist-sized goliath beetle and the Queen Alexandra bird-wing butterfly. This has a wingspan that would reach from the top to the bottom of this page.**

The most massive living insects are the goliath beetles of Africa. They weigh up to 100 grams and can measure up to ten centimetres long. Some of the scarabs, dung beetles and the rhinoceros beetles are only slightly smaller.

The titan beetle of Brazil is one of the longhorn beetles. It grows to 15 centimetres in length and many stick insects are even longer. The world's longest insect is an Indonesian species that reaches over 30 centimetres in length.

Butterflies and moths have the largest wings and the world's largest butterfly is the Queen Alexandra birdwing butterfly of New Guinea. Females have wingspans of over 28 centimetres.

## ▼ WHICH WERE THE LARGEST INSECTS OF ALL?

**The largest known insect lived 280 million years ago in the steamy swamp forests of the Carboniferous period. It is known as *Meganeura monyi*.**

Insects cannot grow beyond a certain size. A human-sized insect, for example, would be impossible. It would not be able to take in enough oxygen and, in any case, its body would probably be crushed by air pressure.

Even so, some of the earliest insects were much larger than those of today. The largest were the giant dragonflies *(Meganeura)*, which had wingspans of up to 70 centimetres.

These insects could reach such a size because there were no predators in the air and they did not have to compete with other animals for food.

Today such insects would make easy prey for birds. And they would find it difficult to compete for food with all the insects, birds and mammals that feed in the trees.

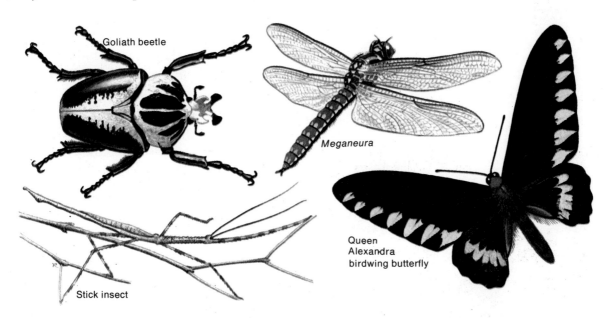

Goliath beetle

Meganeura

Stick insect

Queen Alexandra birdwing butterfly

## ▼ WHAT ARE SOCIAL INSECTS?

**Most insects live alone. But a few species live in groups, or colonies. Some colonies are small but others may contain millions of individuals.**

Social insects include some bees, such as honey bees, and some wasps, such as the common wasp. All ants and termites are social insects.

The important fact about social insects is that all the members work for the good of the whole colony. In most colonies there are three or more different types, or castes, of individuals. Each one has a particular task to do.

There are many kinds of colonies. Wasps build complicated nests with many layers in underground chambers or in hollow trees. They use paper, which they make by mixing chewed wood with saliva.

Honey bees build nests of vertical wax sheets, or combs. Termites often build huge, mound-like nests. Many ants dig underground nests.

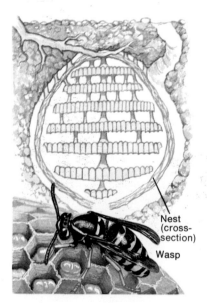

Nest (cross-section)

Wasp

## ▲ HOW MANY BEES LIVE IN A HIVE?

**In the middle of summer a beehive contains one queen, between 50,000 and 60,000 workers and a few hundred males, or drones.**

Queens, workers and drones are the three castes of honey bee. A colony contains only one queen. She lays eggs and her presence controls what the other members of the colony do. Worker bees are all infertile females. Their task is to look after the colony. Drones are fertile males. They are produced only in mid- to late summer. They do no work and their only function is to mate with a queen.

After hatching from her pupa, a worker spends the first two weeks of her life tending and feeding the grubs in their cells. During the third week she helps to build new cells and repair damaged parts of the nest. She also converts nectar into honey. The next three weeks are spent collecting nectar and pollen, after which she dies.

## ▲ HOW FEROCIOUS ARE ARMY ANTS?

**Stories about army ants are often exaggerated. However, any animal that cannot get out of the way of a marching column of army ants will be eaten down to its skeleton in a very short time.**

During the day army ants march in long columns, foraging for food as they go.

The main part of the column consists of between 80,000 and one million small workers, who carry the queen, grubs and pupae. Soldier ants are larger workers with huge heads and jaws. They act as scouts and guards for the column.

At night, the column rests and the workers link their legs to form a temporary nest for the queen and grubs.

Army ants feed mostly on other insects. But any other animal, dead or alive, that they come across is also rapidly devoured. A snake that is too full of food to move quickly will be eaten and a tethered horse stands no chance.

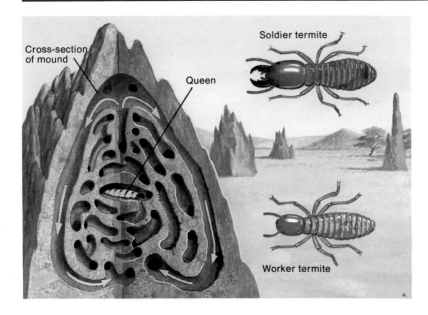

Cross-section of mound

Queen

Soldier termite

Worker termite

## ▲ WHAT HAPPENS INSIDE A TERMITE MOUND?

**Many termites build their nests inside huge mounds. Inside a mound is a network of tunnels and chambers where the workers look after the young.**

A termite mound is begun by a new queen and her king. Later on the workers take over the task of nest-building.

The mound is built of earth and plant material cemented together with saliva and dung. The outer walls are rock hard. But the inside of the mound is like a huge sponge, with thousands of small chambers connected by tiny openings.

Ventilation shafts keep air circulating through the nest. But the atmosphere inside is warm and moist and the carbon dioxide content of the air is unusually high.

The shapes of termite mounds vary. Some are huge towers over three metres high. When land is being cleared for farming, some termite mounds are even too strong for bulldozers, and have to be destroyed by explosives.

## ▲ WHAT ARE SOLDIERS AND WORKERS?

**In any termite nest there are four different castes. The king and queen produce young. Workers tend the nest and soldiers defend it.**

Termites look like ants, but they are not related. Ants are close relatives of bees and wasps, whereas termites are more closely related to cockroaches. Ant workers and soldiers are all infertile females, but in a termite colony they are of both sexes.

Worker termites are the smallest but most numerous members of the colony. Their mouthparts are designed for feeding the queen and her young and for building and repairing the nest.

Soldier termites are much larger. They have huge heads and are often armed with a pair of fearsome jaws. They defend the colony from ants, which are the main enemies of termites. The soldiers of some termites have long snouts instead of jaws. These are used to squirt a sticky liquid at ants.

## ▼ WHAT ARE CATERPILLARS AND NYMPHS?

**Caterpillars and nymphs are both young forms of insects.**

Before becoming adult, a young insect has to go through a series of growth stages. Between each stage the insect moults, or sheds its skin. At the last stage it goes through a change, or metamorphosis, to become an adult.

The young of some insects have growth stages that are similar to the adults. These forms are called nymphs. The nymphs of winged insects are like the adults. But they have wing buds instead of fully-formed wings.

Caterpillars and grubs, on the other hand, are not at all like the adult forms. Their bodies and legs are usually soft and no wings are visible. They also live and feed in a totally different way. The differences are so great that they have to have a special growth stage called the pupa, or chrysalis stage, before they can become adults.

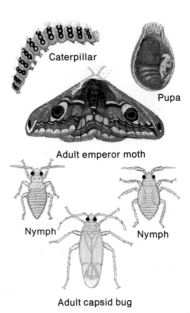

Caterpillar

Pupa

Adult emperor moth

Nymph

Nymph

Adult capsid bug

25

## ▼ WHAT ARE SEA URCHINS AND STARFISH?

**Sea urchins and starfish belong to the group of sea animals known as echinoderms (spiny-skinned animals). This group also includes the sea lilies and sea cucumbers.**

The hard shell, or test, of a sea urchin is formed from a number of chalky plates that lie in its skin. Many of these plates bear long spines.

Other echinoderms also have skeletons made of chalky

## ▼ WHAT ARE SEA SQUIRTS AND LANCELETS?

**Lancelets are small fish-like creatures that live in the mud or sand of shallow water. Sea squirts are bag-like animals that live attached to rocks.**

The lancelet amphioxus is about five centimetres long. It feeds by filtering particles from the water around it. Amphioxus is not a fish. Its body is different in many ways.

In particular, it does not

have a true backbone. Instead it has a long, rod-like structure, or notochord, down its back. A notochord is also found in the early embryos of all vertebrates (animals with backbones). So lancelets and vertebrates are both classified in the group known as the chordates.

Sea squirts are also chordates. At first glance this seems strange because an adult sea squirt is even less like a vertebrate than a lancelet. However, the young larva of a sea squirt does have a notochord.

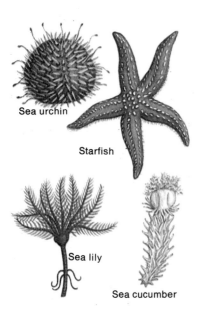

Sea urchin

Starfish

Sea lily

Sea cucumber

Sea squirts

Amphioxus

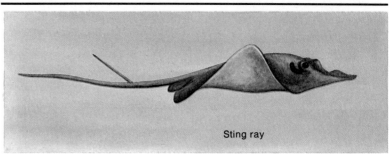

Sting ray

plates. But the plates of starfish are more loosely arranged, so they are flexible animals.

Another feature of the echinoderms is that their bodies are always based on a five-sided plan. This is most easily seen in starfish, which have five arms. But if you examine a sea urchin closely, you will see five rows of tube feet down its sides.

These tube feet are fluid-filled tubes that extend out of the body. They may be used for walking, feeding or taking in oxygen.

## ▲ WHAT ARE SKATES AND RAYS?

**Skates and rays are fishes with flat bodies. Their skeletons are made of cartilage.**

The 'wings' of a ray are formed from the flattened sides of its body and the greatly enlarged pectoral, or shoulder, fins. It swims by passing waves along its wings.

Most skates and rays feed on shrimps, shellfish and crabs, which they crush with their powerful jaws. Many of

the smaller species hide from predators by lying camouflaged on the sea bed. A sting ray defends itself with a poison spine on its tail.

Manta rays, or devil fish, have wingspans of up to seven metres. They are harmless plankton feeders. Electric rays are carnivores. They stun their prey with their electric organs.

The shark-like sawfish uses its saw for digging up shellfish. But it will also flail its saw from side to side in a shoal of fish and then feed on the injured fish.

### ▼ WHAT IS A SHARK?

**Sharks, like skates and rays, have skeletons made of cartilage. Most sharks are predatory and have many sharp teeth.**

Sharks are closely related to the skates and rays. They are streamlined fishes designed for fast swimming.

Unlike a bony fish, a shark has no swim bladder to keep it buoyant in the water. Instead, the shape of its head, its wing-like fins and its upturned tail all help to provide lift as the shark swims. Some sharks increase their buoyancy by storing oil in their livers.

A shark's skin is covered in thousands of tiny, pointed scales. These continue into the mouth, where they are larger and form many rows of sharp teeth. These are used for holding and tearing the flesh of prey. The shark swallows pieces of prey whole.

The smallest sharks are the harmless dogfish, which scavenge for food on the sea bed. Other sharks are fierce predators.

### ▼ HOW DANGEROUS ARE SHARKS?

**All large flesh-eating sharks may attack humans. But stories of man-eating sharks are often greatly exaggerated.**

Most sharks are not really dangerous and do not always attack. But it is wise to get out of the water when a shark is nearby. Sand sharks and hammerhead sharks have been known to attack bathers. Grey reef sharks sometimes attack divers, and seafarers used to fear mackerel sharks. The great white shark sometimes grows to over ten metres long. It is a terrifying predator.

Other dangerous sharks include the porbeagle, tiger shark and the great blue shark. Makos, the fastest of all sharks, sometimes attack small boats.

Splashing the water to drive sharks away is a mistake. Sharks feed on sick or wounded prey and may mistake a human for a dying fish. Splashing only adds to this impression.

### ▼ WHICH IS THE LARGEST FISH OF ALL?

**The world's largest fish is the whale shark. But far from being a man-eater, this fish is a completely harmless plankton feeder.**

Whale sharks are found in tropical waters. Most are about 15 metres long, but a record specimen caught in 1919 was 18.5 metres long.

A whale shark feeds by sieving plankton from the water. Inside its mouth its gill arches bear a number of 'strainers', or gill rakers. These collect up plankton and small fishes from the water that passes into the fish's mouth and out through its gills.

Basking sharks are also large sharks, reaching lengths of up to 12 metres. They are plankton feeders like whale sharks, but they are found in colder waters. Their food consists of small, shrimp-like animals, fish eggs and arrow worms. During winter when food is scarce, they lose their gill rakers and stop feeding.

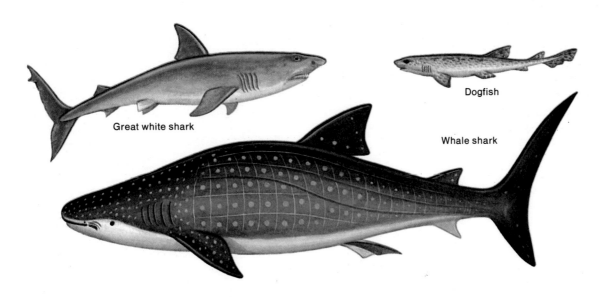

Great white shark

Dogfish

Whale shark

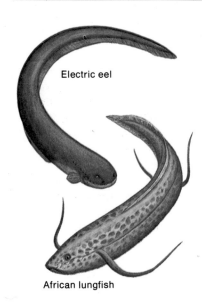

Electric eel

African lungfish

## ▲ WHICH FISHES BREATHE AIR?

**Lungfishes are able to breathe air and survive out of water.**

The swim bladders of bony fishes originally evolved as simple lungs. Many early fishes lived in stagnant swamps. There was not much oxygen and so the ability to breathe air was an advantage. Most modern fishes live where there is plenty of oxygen and so do not need to breathe air.

Lungfishes have kept their lungs. Some lungfishes can survive without water in times of drought. Other fishes with lungs include bichirs, gar-pikes and the bowfin.

Some fishes, such as the catfish *Clarias*, have special gills that do not collapse in air and can take in oxygen. Another catfish, called *Hoplosternum*, gulps mouthfuls of air and takes in oxygen through the lining of its gut.

The electric eel can breathe through the lining of its mouth. So can the mudskipper, which spends much of its time out of water.

## ▼ WHAT IS A BONY FISH?

**Bony fishes have skeletons made mostly of bone rather than cartilage. They are the true masters of the world's seas and rivers.**

Bony fishes have become adapted to a wide variety of lifestyles. There are at present about 18,000 species.

The body of a bony fish contains a swim bladder. This is a gas-filled bag that helps it to float at any level in the water. The body of a typical bony fish is flattened from side to side and is used in swimming.

Most bony fishes use their fins for steering and braking, although some species use their fins as oars to 'row' them through the water.

The shapes and colours of bony fishes depend on their ways of life. Predatory fishes, such as swordfish and tuna, are streamlined, fast swimmers. Flatfish are camouflaged on the sea bed, while brightly coloured fishes live around equally brightly coloured coral reefs.

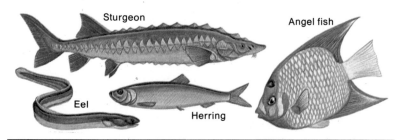

Sturgeon

Angel fish

Eel

Herring

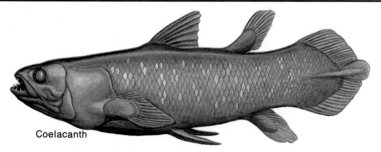

Coelacanth

## ▲ WHAT IS A COELACANTH?

**The coelacanth is a 'living fossil'. It is a type of fish that has remained unchanged for millions of years.**

Until 1938, scientists believed that the coelacanth had been extinct for 70 million years. Since then over 80 specimens have been caught near the Comoro Islands off the East Africa coast.

Coelacanths belong to the group of fishes known as lobe-fins, which have fins supported on fleshy lobes. This group also includes the lung-fishes and the extinct rhipidistians, which lived about 370 million years ago and were probably the ancestors of the first amphibians.

The coelacanth is something of a puzzle. Its body has unusual features. For example, it has a notochord instead of a backbone and its heart and stomach are very simple. There seems to be no reason why this fish should have survived for so long with so little change.

### ▼ WHAT KIND OF ANIMAL IS A SEAHORSE?

**These strange sea creatures, that look like the knights in a game of chess, are in fact bony fishes.**

Seahorses are well named. The large heads of these fishes look amazingly like horses' heads.

Seahorses vary in size and colour, but they all have the same basic shape. When resting, a seahorse wraps its tail round a piece of seaweed.

It swims in an upright position, using its dorsal fin to drive it along. The fin vibrates very rapidly (up to 35 times a second), but the seahorse actually swims rather slowly.

Seahorses are unusual in another way – the males produce the young. A male seahorse has a pouch on its belly. During courtship, the female places her eggs into this pouch and the male then fertilizes them. When the eggs hatch out, the male, with a series of jerks, shoots the young out one by one.

### ▼ WHICH FISHES LIVE DEEP IN THE OCEANS?

**Many strange fishes inhabit the Earth's deep waters. They are adapted for life in a dark world where food may be scarce.**

Most sea animals live in the upper layers of the oceans. Light can easily get through and there is plenty of food.

Below 500 metres, however, in the bathypelagic zone, the water becomes darker and food is scarce. Fishes that live in this zone have become adapted to making the most of the occasional prey they can find. Viper fish, bristlemouths, hatchet fish and angler fish all have large mouths for swallowing prey rapidly.

At the bottom of the sea, in the abyssal zone, food is actually more plentiful. It consists of dead plankton and other animals.

The most common fishes of these totally dark depths are rat tails and deep-sea cods. Among the predators there are deep-sea angler fish. Gulper fish and swallowers can swallow very large prey.

### ▼ WHICH FISHES CARRY THEIR OWN LIGHTS?

**Many deep-sea fishes have light-producing organs. These may help fishes to recognize their own kind and they may act as lures for prey.**

Lantern fish have rows of light-producing organs down their sides which can be switched on and off. These organs may be used as a means of communication and to help lantern fish to recognize members of their own species.

At night, lantern fish rise closer to the surface to feed on small animals. Their light-producing organs may act as lures. Deep-sea angler fish have luminous lures.

Other deep-sea fishes that have light-producing organs include viperfish, bristle-mouths and hatchet fish. The organs of a hatchet fish are arranged along its belly. They appear to help to camouflage the fish. The light shining down from its belly matches the light coming from above and the fish does not appear as a dark shadow from below.

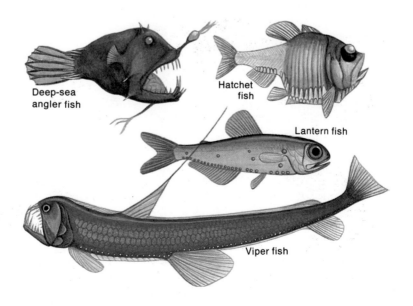

Deep-sea angler fish

Hatchet fish

Lantern fish

Viper fish

### ▼ WHAT ARE NEWTS AND SALAMANDERS?

**Newts and salamanders are amphibians. They are four-legged animals with long bodies and moist skin.**

A salamander has a long tail and four limbs held out sideways from its long body. Its soft, moist skin tends to lose water easily and so salamanders have to live in water or in damp places.

Salamanders lay soft eggs without shells. Usually they lay these in water to prevent them from drying out. The eggs hatch out into larvae, which use gills to obtain oxygen. After a time, a larva goes through a change, or metamorphosis. It loses its gills and other larval features to become an adult with lungs.

Most salamanders spend at least part of their lives on land. But a few never leave the water. The Mexican axolotl never even reaches true adulthood. It is able to breed while still keeping its gills and other larval features.

### ▼ WHAT ARE FROGS AND TOADS?

**Frogs and toads form the largest group of amphibians. Some live in water, but most are land-dwellers.**

Adult frogs and toads have short bodies, well-developed hind legs and no tails. Frogs are usually slender animals. They have large eyes and are extremely agile. Toads are heavier and clumsier. Land-dwelling toads often have dry skins.

Common frogs, common toads and many others are ground-dwellers that live in woods and fields. A few toads, such as the South African clawed toad and the Surinam toad, live in water all the time. Tree frogs have toe pads that enable them to climb.

The young of frogs and toads hatch out from the eggs as tadpoles, which later undergo metamorphosis to become adults. Most frogs and toads lay their eggs in water. But the male midwife toad carries the eggs in strings wrapped round his legs.

### ▼ WHICH ARE THE LARGEST AMPHIBIANS?

**The world's largest amphibian is the Chinese giant salamander. The largest frog is the goliath frog of Africa and the largest toad is the marine toad of South America.**

Giant salamanders, or hellbenders, are found in China, Japan and North America. Most are over one metre in length and some Chinese giant salamanders grow to over three and a half metres long. They are carnivorous amphibians that live in fast-flowing mountain streams.

Giant frogs, or goliath frogs, are found in tropical West Africa. Their bodies may be up to 34 centimetres long and can weigh over three kilograms. They live near waterfalls and are excellent swimmers.

The marine toad is a native amphibian of tropical South and Central America. Adults can grow to about 24 centimetres in length and may weigh up to 1300 grams.

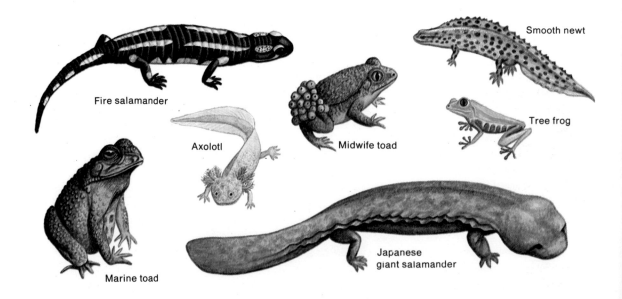

Fire salamander

Smooth newt

Axolotl

Midwife toad

Tree frog

Marine toad

Japanese giant salamander

## ▼ WHAT ARE TURTLES AND TORTOISES?

**Turtles and tortoises are reptiles. Their bodies are encased in hard shells.**

The shell of a turtle or tortoise is made up of a number of bony plates that lock together. Turtles and tortoises have no teeth, unlike most reptiles. Instead they have sharp, horny beaks.

There are two main groups of turtles. One group contains those that withdraw their heads by bending their necks

## ▼ WHAT ARE LIZARDS?

**Lizards are long-bodied reptiles. The group includes geckos, iguanas, chameleons and skinks.**

Like all reptiles, lizards have scaly skins and lay hard-shelled eggs on land. They are closely related to the snakes. But, unlike a snake, a lizard has movable eyelids and an eardrum just behind its lower jaw. And, of course, most lizards have four legs.

Almost all lizards live entirely on land. Many are

fast runners and some can run on their hind legs. The basilisk can run so fast that it is able to run across water.

Typical lizards include the common lizard and the green lizard. The most numerous lizards are the skinks, which have fat bodies. The smallest lizards are geckos. A few species measure just three and a half centimetres long.

Other groups of lizards include the agamids, the iguanas and the chameleons. Lizards without legs include the slow-worm and the worm-lizards, or amphisbaenids.

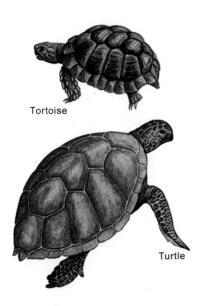

Tortoise

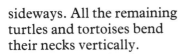

Turtle

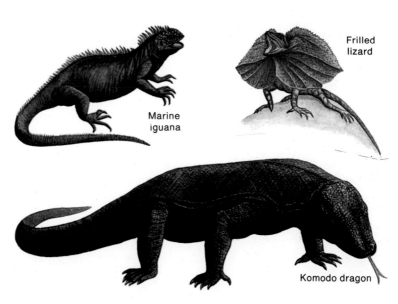

Marine iguana

Frilled lizard

Komodo dragon

sideways. All the remaining turtles and tortoises bend their necks vertically.

Tortoises are land-dwellers. They have rounded shells like domes and well-developed legs. The largest are the Galapagos tortoises, which can grow to one and a half metres long.

Most freshwater turtles spend part of their time out of water. Sea turtles, on the other hand, only leave the sea to lay eggs. They have powerful paddles that are used like 'wings' for flying through the water.

## ▲ WHAT IS A KOMODO DRAGON?

**The Komodo dragon is the largest lizard in the world. In fact it is the largest land lizard that has ever existed.**

The Komodo dragon belongs to the family of monitor lizards, several of which are large animals. Nile monitors can measure over two metres long and the Komodo dragon can be over three metres long.

Although the Komodo dragon looks like a relic of the

age of dinosaurs, it is in fact a true lizard. The only larger lizards that have ever existed were the ten-metre-long mosasaurs that lived in the seas 100 million years ago.

Komodo dragons are found only on the island of Komodo and a few other Indonesian islands. They feed on carrion but will also kill large animals.

A Komodo dragon tears off large chunks of meat and swallows them whole. It can devour a whole deer or goat in about ten minutes and then go for several days without food.

Boa constrictor

Grass snake

## ◄ WHAT ARE SNAKES?

**Snakes are long, legless reptiles closely related to the lizards. They probably evolved from a group of lizards that took up a burrowing way of life.**

All snakes are carnivorous (flesh-eaters). Some, such as grass snakes, catch their prey simply by seizing it in their sharp teeth. However, a snake's jaws are too weak to catch large prey in this way. Many snakes are poisonous. To kill large prey, they inject it with venom.

Other snakes, such as boas and pythons, kill their prey by crushing it. As the coils squeeze tighter, the prey cannot breathe and dies of suffocation.

Snakes swallow their prey whole. They are able to do this because their jaws can be separated to allow the prey to pass down the throat. An egg-eating snake can eat an egg four times as wide as its own body. The reticulated python, which is the world's largest snake (up to ten metres long), can swallow a large bush pig.

## ▼ WHAT WERE DINOSAURS?

**Dinosaurs were reptiles that dominated the world for 150 million years. There were many types, including huge plant-eaters and fierce carnivores. But by 65 million years ago all the dinosaurs had died out.**

Dinosaurs ruled the world during the Mesozoic, or 'middle life' era. This is divided into three periods: the Triassic, Jurassic and Cretaceous.

The ancestors of dinosaurs were reptiles that ran on their hind legs. As a result, many dinosaurs also walked or ran on their hind legs.

Dinosaurs belong to two separate reptile groups. The saurischians had lizard-like hip bones. This group included the huge plant-eating sauropods and the terrifying carnosaurs. The ornithischians had bird-like hip bones. This group included ornithopods, stegosaurs, the ankylosaurs and the ceratopsians.

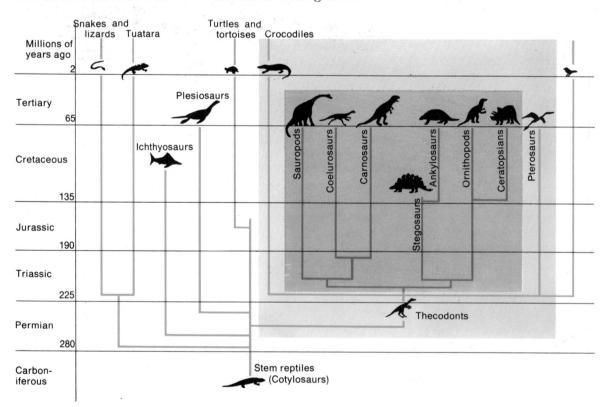

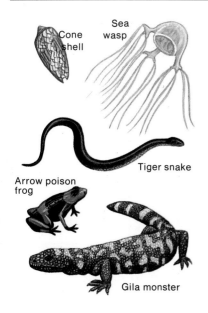

Crocodile

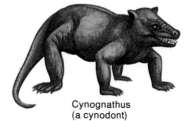

Cynognathus
(a cynodont)

Alligator

Lycaenops

## ▲ WHICH ANIMALS ARE THE MOST POISONOUS?

**Poisonous snakes are well known. But there are also poisonous kinds of fishes, lizards, amphibians and invertebrate animals.**

The world's most poisonous land snakes are the fierce snake and the tiger snake, both of Australia. Just 100 milligrams of venom from a fierce snake is enough to kill over 100,000 mice. But the sea snake *Hydrophis belcheri* is even more poisonous.

The only two poisonous lizards, the gila monster and the beaded lizard, are mildly poisonous.

The marine toad produces poison from two glands on its head and arrow poison frogs produce a lethal poison on their skin. Several fishes defend themselves with poison spines. The deadliest of these are the stonefishes.

Some deadly poisonous invertebrates include the blue-ringed octopus and cone shells. The sting of a sea wasp, an Australian relative of jellyfish, can kill a person within two minutes.

## ▲ WHAT IS THE DIFFERENCE BETWEEN CROCODILES AND ALLIGATORS?

**When a crocodile closes its jaws, the fourth tooth of the lower jaw can still be seen. In alligators and their relatives, the tooth fits into a pit in the upper jaw and cannot be seen.**

Crocodiles and their relatives are divided into three families, but there are very few differences between them

As well as the difference in their teeth, they have slightly different scale patterns and differently shaped snouts. Most true crocodiles have long, broad snouts. Alligators and caimans have shorter snouts and gavials have very long, narrow snouts.

Crocodiles and alligators lay their eggs on land. But they spend a lot of time keeping cool in water.

They lie in wait for their prey, which consists of fishes and other small animals. Occasionally, large crocodiles may catch quite large mammals that come to the water to drink.

## ▲ WHAT WERE THE MAMMAL-LIKE REPTILES?

**Mammal-like reptiles lived between about 290 and 220 million years ago. They were the ancestors of the true mammals.**

Mammal-like reptiles were the dominant animals on Earth during the period of time known as the Permian period. Many of them had features that are found today in mammals.

The earliest types were the pelycosaurs. This group included the strange 'sail-backs', such as *Edaphosaurus*.

About 250 million years ago the pelycosaurs were replaced by the therapsids. This was a very varied group. It included the dinocephalians ('big heads'), such as *Moschops*, the dicynodonts, which had turtle-like jaws, and the fierce gorgonopsians, such as *Lycaenops*.

About 220 million years ago, when most mammal-like reptiles had died out, the cynodonts still dominated the land. This group probably gave rise to the first tiny, shrew-like mammals.

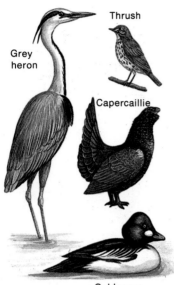

Thrush

Grey heron

Capercaillie

Goldeneye

Rhea

King penguin

Kiwi

Brown-throated spinetail swift

Peregrine falcon

### ◀ WHAT IS A BIRD?

**Birds are warm-blooded vertebrates (animals with backbones). They have feathers to keep them warm. They walk on their hind legs and their front limbs are wings.**

A bird's body is designed for flying. It is compact and light, but at the same time it is very strong. Lightness is achieved in several ways. The skull, for example, has fewer bones than the skulls of other vertebrates and the jaws are small and do not carry teeth. The larger bones of the body are hollow, reinforced inside with cross-struts. Some bones are fused together for strength.

A bird's wings are mostly made up of feathers. These are supported on the greatly lengthened bones of the 'arm' and 'hand'. The large breast bone, or sternum, has powerful wing muscles attached.

Flying uses up a large amount of oxygen. So a bird has eight air sacs that supply its lungs with a continuous stream of air.

### ◀ WHICH BIRDS CANNOT FLY?

**Some birds, such as the ostrich and emu, have lost the ability to fly. The wings of penguins are used for swimming instead of flying.**

Flightless birds are found in a number of places. The ostrich roams the African savannah and the two species of rhea live in the grasslands of South America. Emus and takahes are Australian birds. Cassowaries are also found in northern Australia and New Guinea. Kiwis live in the forests of New Zealand.

Most flightless birds live where there are few natural enemies. But they have no protection against introduced predators and human hunters.

Penguins are found in the colder regions of the southern hemisphere. They are different from other flightless birds because their wings are far from useless. They are very efficient flippers and penguins are superb swimmers.

### ◀ WHICH BIRDS ARE THE FASTEST FLIERS?

**Swifts are among the fastest of all flying birds. Other fast fliers include peregrine falcons, swallows and homing pigeons.**

The fastest known bird in level flight is the white-throated spinetail swift. It has been recorded as flying at speeds of over 170 kilometres an hour (km/h). Peregrine falcons can chase their prey in level flight at 60 km/h, but when stooping, or diving, on prey they reach much higher speeds. There are claims of stooping peregrines achieving speeds of between 290 and 350 km/h.

Other high-speed birds include buzzards, which can glide at between 110 and 130 km/h. Swallows are believed to be able to reach 160 km/h when migrating, but they do not normally fly faster than about 50 km/h.

Speeds of up to 80 km/h have been recorded for house martins and homing pigeons.

### ▶ WHAT IS A BIRD OF PREY?

**Birds of prey are those that hunt live animals. They have sharp talons (claws) on their feet and large, hooked beaks.**

Almost all birds of prey catch and kill their own food. They use their sharp talons for grasping their prey and they tear the flesh with their strong, hooked beaks.

There are over 250 species of birds of prey. They include all the eagles, hawks, kites, buzzards and falcons. Small birds of prey, such as the kestrel (one of the falcons), prey on small animals, amphibians and insects. Larger types prey on birds and larger mammals. The harpy eagle, the world's largest bird of prey, lives on monkeys, squirrels and birds.

Several birds of prey specialize in particular kinds of animal. The osprey and the African fish eagle feed only on fish. The secretary bird of South America catches only reptiles. The Everglades kite feeds on a freshwater snail.

Golden eagle

### ▶ WHICH BIRDS HUNT AT NIGHT?

**Almost all owls are night-hunters. They have good night vision and exceptionally good hearing.**

Like birds of prey, owls have sharp talons and hooked beaks for catching and eating live animals. A few, such as the short-eared owl and the snowy owl, hunt both at night and during the day. But most owls hunt only at night.

Owls have large, forward-pointing eyes that help them to see well in the dark. But the owl uses sound to find its prey. Its ears are surrounded by small flaps of skin which help to collect sounds. The arrangement of the feathers on and around the face is also thought to help in hearing.

Most owls make their nests in trees, either in holes or in the abandoned nests of other birds. However, a few owls, such as the short-eared owl and the snowy owl, nest on the ground. The rare burrowing owl of western America makes its nest in a hole in the ground.

Sparrowhawk

Tawny owl

### ▶ WHICH BIRD HAS THE LONGEST WINGSPAN?

**Albatrosses have long, thin wings for gliding. The bird with the longest wingspan is the wandering albatross.**

Wandering albatrosses soar across the southern oceans, feeding on fish and other sea animals near the surface. They cover enormous distances with very little effort.

Their long, thin wings are designed for fast gliding.

Fully spread, the wings of a wandering albatross measure over three metres from wingtip to wingtip. The greatest recorded wingspan is 3.63 metres. Such wings provide only a small amount of lift. But this does not matter, as this bird lives in an area where there is almost always enough wind to provide the lift it needs.

Wandering albatrosses nest on the tops of cliffs. From there, they can usually take off from the cliff edge into upcurrents of air.

Wandering albatross

### ◀ WHICH MAMMALS LAY EGGS?

**The duck-billed platypus and the five species of spiny anteaters, or echidnas, are egg-laying mammals. Together they form the group known as the monotremes.**

All mammals are warm-blooded, hairy-skinned animals that feed their new-born young on milk produced by mammary glands. Most mammals nourish their developing young inside the female's body. But monotremes lay eggs.

The platypus lives in slow-moving rivers in western Australia. After mating, a female platypus lays two eggs in a burrow and tends them for about ten days until they hatch. Then she suckles her young with milk.

A female echidna lays her single egg into a pouch, which develops on her belly at the start of each breeding season. In about ten days the young echidna hatches and sucks milk from tufts of fur inside the pouch.

### ▶ WHAT ARE POUCHED MAMMALS?

**Mammals that have pouches for rearing their young are known as marsupials. They are all found in South America or Australia, except one.**

A young marsupial is nourished in its mother's womb by only a very simple placenta and does not stay in the womb for long. It is born in a very underdeveloped state, and continues to grow in its mother's pouch.

Australian marsupials include kangaroos, wallabies and koalas. There are also the possums, phalangers, wombats, bandicoots, the marsupial mole and the numbat, which does not have a pouch. Marsupial carnivores include the Tasmanian devil, the native-cats and marsupial mice.

South American marsupials include the water opossum and the mouse opossums, which do not have pouches. The only marsupial found in North America is the Virginia opossum.

Virginia opossum

Koala

### ◀ WHAT ARE PLACENTAL MAMMALS?

**Placental mammals form the largest group of mammals. A female placental mammal nourishes her young for some time in her womb by means of an organ called a placenta.**

Placental mammals are the most advanced type of mammals. A young placental mammal stays in its mother's womb until it is fairly well developed. The all-important placenta keeps it supplied with food and oxygen and removes the young mammal's waste material. The placenta brings the bloodstreams of the mother and young close together without the blood actually mixing.

There are 18 orders, or groups, of placental mammals. The smallest group contains just one species – the aardvark. Colugos (flying lemurs), elephant shrews and tree shrews form three other small orders. The largest is that of the rodents, with over 1600 species.

## ▶ WHAT DO HEDGEHOGS, MOLES AND SHREWS HAVE IN COMMON?

**Hedgehogs, moles and shrews all belong to the mammal order Insectivora. This name means 'insect-eaters', but insects form only part of the diet of these animals.**

Hedgehogs are omnivorous animals. They feed not only on insects but also on worms, snails and plant material, such as berries and acorns. Sometimes they take the eggs of wild birds.

Moles live and feed underground. They do eat insects but their main source of food is earthworms. Moles are well adapted for their underground way of life. They have large front limbs for digging and their short fur can be brushed in any direction.

Shrews are the smallest and most numerous insectivores. They feed on insects and other animals, and a shrew has to eat its own weight in food every 24 hours. Some shrews will even kill and eat rodents their own size.

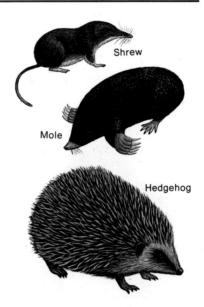

Shrew

Mole

Hedgehog

## ◀ WHICH MAMMALS FLY IN THE DARK?

**The only true flying mammals are the bats. All bats fly at night and most feed on insects.**

A bat's wing is formed from a large membrane supported by both the front and hind limbs and by four long 'fingers' of its 'hand'. Other 'flying' mammals, such as flying squirrels, can only glide, but a bat actually flies.

Most bats eat insects. They are able to find their prey and avoid obstacles in the dark by using sound waves (echolocation). A bat catches an insect in its wing membrane and then transfers it to its mouth.

However, not all bats eat insects. Vampire bats feed on the blood of large mammals. One false vampire bat preys on lizards, smaller bats, birds and mice.

Some tropical bats have extra-long tongues for drinking nectar from flowers. Others eat fruit and flowers. The best known fruit-eating bat is the flying fox.

Flying fox

Noctule bat

## ▶ WHAT ARE PRIMATES?

**The mammal order primates includes the lemurs and their relatives, monkeys, apes and man.**

All primates have five fingers and toes and can grasp objects with their hands (and often their feet). They have good colour vision and use sight rather than smell to find food and spot predators.

The lemurs, bushbabies, tarsiers and lorises are some of the most primitive primates. Monkeys are divided into two main groups. The New World monkeys of tropical America have broad, flat noses and widely-spaced nostrils. They include the marmosets, spider monkeys, howler monkeys, capuchins and douroucoulis. Most of these have grasping tails.

Old World monkeys, such as colobuses, langurs, guenons, macaques and baboons, only use their tails for balancing.

Apes include the gibbons, the orang-utan, gorilla and chimpanzee. Apes are found only in Asia and Africa.

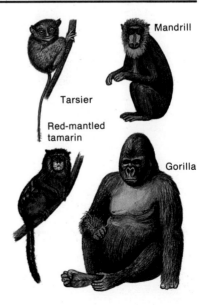

Mandrill

Tarsier

Red-mantled tamarin

Gorilla

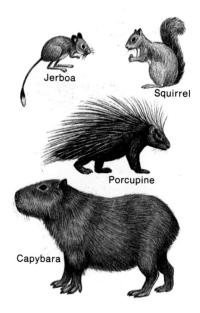

Jerboa

Squirrel

Porcupine

Capybara

Hare

Rabbit

## ▲ WHAT ARE RODENTS?

**Rodents are mammals with chisel-like incisor (cutting) teeth at the front of their jaws. These teeth grow continuously as they are worn down.**

All rodents gnaw their food with their two pairs of front teeth. Between these teeth and the grinding teeth at the back of the jaw there is a gap. When a rodent is gnawing at inedible material, such as wood, it can close off its mouth by pushing its cheek folds into the gap.

Rodents are plant-eaters, although they sometimes eat snails and insects. Most use their front paws to hold their food while they eat. And most are burrowing animals.

Rodents include mice, rats, voles and tree squirrels. Also in this group are the beavers, porcupines, jerboas, kangaroo rats and ground squirrels, such as prairie dogs.

The largest rodent is the South American capybara, which is the size of a small pig. This creature lives in water, rather like a hippopotamus.

## ▲ WHAT IS THE DIFFERENCE BETWEEN A RABBIT AND A HARE?

**Rabbits raise their young in burrows. Hares raise their young in the open.**

Rabbits and hares belong to the mammal order Lagomorpha. They are like rodents because they have gnawing incisor teeth that grow continuously. But lagomorphs have four incisor teeth in their upper jaws while rodents have only two.

Rabbits build warm nests in burrows. Their young are born blind and without fur and remain in the nest for about a month. A newly-born leveret (young hare), on the other hand, has fully-opened eyes and is covered in soft fur. To begin with, young leverets are left in their 'forms', which are just depressions in the grass. But they can fend for themselves much sooner than young rabbits.

The true rabbit is a native of Europe and North Africa. Hares include the brown hare and alpine hare of Europe, and the snowshoe rabbit and jackrabbit of North America.

## ▼ WHAT IS AN ARMADILLO?

**Armadillos are armoured mammals found in South America.**

Most mammals have soft skins covered in fur or hair. They rely on their speed, or their ability to hide, to escape from predators. Armadillos, however, have developed armour for protection.

The armour consists of bony plates that cover the animal's back and sides. Some species can roll themselves into a ball. Others just pull in their feet and crouch. If attacked, they can also fight fiercely with their sharp claws.

Armadillos eat a variety of small animals, such as insects (especially ants and termites), worms and lizards. The nine-banded armadillo is the most common. It is the only one found in North America.

South American armadillos include the smaller six-banded armadillo, the rat-sized fairy armadillo and the hairy armadillo. The largest is the giant armadillo, which may be a metre long.

## ▼ WHAT ARE ANTEATERS AND SLOTHS?

**Anteaters and sloths are relatives of the armadillos. Anteaters are ground-dwellers that feed on ants and termites. Sloths spend their lives hanging in trees.**

Armadillos, anteaters and sloths make up the mammal order known as the edentates. This name means 'without teeth', but this is only true of the anteaters. Armadillos and sloths do have some teeth.

Anteaters live entirely on ants and termites. They tear open nests with their sharp claws and reach deep inside with their long tongues. Anteaters are found only in South America. The giant anteater may measure two metres from head to tail and its tongue may be 90 centimetres long.

Sloths are slow-moving inhabitants of the rain forests of South and Central America. They spend all their lives hanging upside down in trees, feeding on leaves and fruit.

Two-toed sloth

Giant anteater

## ▲ WHAT IS A PANGOLIN?

**Pangolins are a small group of South African and Asian mammals. Most of a pangolin's body is covered in horny scales.**

Pangolins form a mammal order (the Pholidota) on their own. A pangolin has overlapping scales in place of most of its fur. Only the underside of its body is hairy.

The giant pangolin and Temmink's pangolin are the largest members of the order. They can measure up to 170 centimetres, including a 70-centimetre tail.

They and the Indian pangolin are all ground-dwellers. Like anteaters they use their sharp claws and long tongues to feed on termites and ants. The remaining four species are all tree-dwellers and feed mostly on tree ants.

A pangolin's scales help to protect it from the attacks of ants and soldier termites. They can also close their nostrils and their eyes are protected by thick eyelids.

The pangolin swallows pebbles to grind up the ants in its stomach.

## ▲ WHAT IS AN AARDVARK?

**The aardvark is an African mammal that lives mostly on termites. It looks similar to an anteater, but is not closely related to it.**

The aardvark is the only member of the mammal order Tubulidentata ('tube teeth'). This order takes its name from the aardvark's peculiar and unique teeth. They have no enamel on the outside, no roots and they contain many fine tubes.

Like anteaters, the aardvark has a long nose. However, its ears are much larger than an anteater's and its nose ends in a snout, like a pig. *Aardvark* is the Afrikaans word for 'earth pig'. A fully grown aardvark can measure about 180 centimetres long from nose to tail.

Aardvarks are seldom seen. They feed at night and lead secretive lives. Like other termite-eaters, they have strong limbs, sharp claws and long tongues. They also feed on other soft-bodied insects and fruit, but they cannot digest ants.

### ▼ WHAT IS A CARNIVORE?

**The word *carnivore* means 'flesh-eater' and there are many carnivores in the animal kingdom. Some belong to the mammal order Carnivora.**

Some of the best-known members of the Carnivora belong to the cat family. This includes the lion, tiger, leopard, cheetah and jaguar, as well as a number of smaller cats, such as the European wild cat.

The dog family includes the wolf, coyote, dingo, jackals and foxes. Hyenas belong to a separate family.

The weasel family includes the skunk, sable and mink, as well as weasels, polecats, badgers and otters. Civets, mongooses and genets belong to another family.

Other Carnivora include the seals, sea lions and the walrus. Bears and raccoons, which include coatis and the red panda, eat a great deal of plant material. The giant panda, which may be a relative of the bears, lives entirely on bamboo shoots.

### ▼ WHICH IS THE FASTEST LAND ANIMAL?

**The world's fastest land animal is the cheetah, which can run at speeds of up to 100 kilometres an hour. However, it cannot run very far at this speed.**

Some mammals can run swiftly over fairly long distances. Pronghorn antelopes can travel at more than 55 kilometres an hour for over one and a half kilometres.

Cats, on the other hand, cannot run very far. They hunt by stalking their prey. They get as close as possible and then rush over the last few metres. Cats that hunt in open country cannot get very close to their prey, so the last rush has to be very fast. Lions, which often hunt in groups, can reach speeds of up to 65 kilometres an hour.

Cheetahs hunt alone, and can chase their prey at even higher speeds. However, if a cheetah does not catch its intended victim within a few hundred metres, it becomes exhausted and gives up.

### ▼ WHICH ARE THE LARGEST CARNIVORES?

**Kodiak bears and polar bears are the largest land carnivores.**

There are several examples of large carnivores in the world. The largest cat is the Siberian tiger. An adult male can measure over three metres from nose to tail and stand over one metre high at the shoulder.

The largest wild member of the dog family is the grey wolf, but there are taller and heavier breeds of domestic dog.

The bear family contains the largest carnivores. There are several races of brown bear. The fierce grizzly bear is one North American race. The Kodiak bear, on Kodiak Island off the coast of Alaska, is another. The average adult male measures about two and a half metres from head to tail and may weigh over 500 kilograms. Most polar bears are under 400 kilograms in weight. But there are claims of some weighing 800 or even 1000 kilograms.

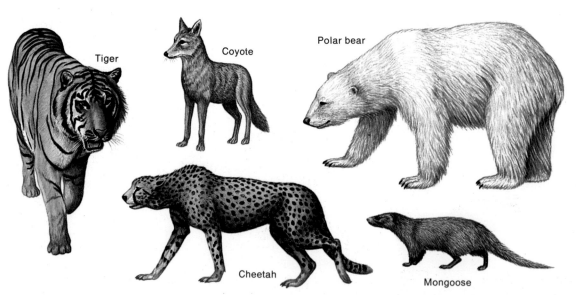

Tiger

Coyote

Polar bear

Cheetah

Mongoose

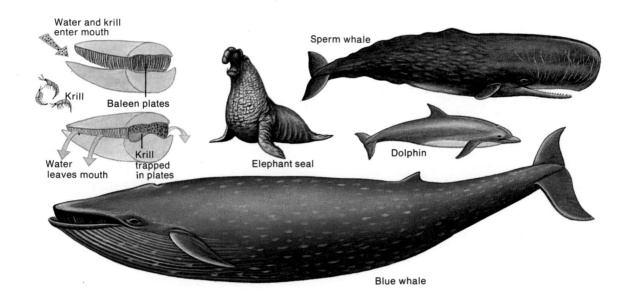

Water and krill enter mouth

Krill

Baleen plates

Water leaves mouth

Krill trapped in plates

Sperm whale

Elephant seal

Dolphin

Blue whale

### ▲ WHICH MAMMALS LIVE IN THE SEA?

**Seals, dolphins and whales are all sea mammals. Seals breed on land, but dolphins and whales never leave the water.**

Dolphins and whales make up the mammal order Cetacea. In spite of their fish-like appearance, they are true placental mammals.

They are well adapted for life in water. They have streamlined bodies, paddles instead of front legs and horizontal tail fins, or flukes, instead of hind legs. Instead of nostrils, a dolphin has a blow-hole on the top of its head that can be closed when the animal is underwater.

Seals and sea lions are members of the order Carnivora. Like most mammals, they are covered in fur, but this lies flat on their streamlined bodies. Their limbs have become flippers, but, unlike dolphins, they can use their front flippers for crawling. Sea lions and fur seals can also use their hind flippers for moving on land.

### ▲ WHICH IS THE BIGGEST LIVING ANIMAL?

**The largest animal that has ever lived on Earth is the blue whale. The largest specimen ever recorded was 33.58 metres long.**

Most whales and dolphins are quite small animals, but a few are enormous. Land animals the size of the blue whale have never existed because they could never support the weight of their bodies. A beached whale cannot breathe because its tremendous weight prevents it from expanding its lungs. Usually the whale's mass is supported by the water around it.

The largest toothed whale is the sperm whale, so called because of the large amounts of spermaceti (a valuable oil) stored in its barrel-shaped head. Bull sperm whales can measure up to 20 metres long and weigh over 50 tonnes.

But even this large animal is dwarfed by the enormous blue whale. A female blue whale can measure over 30 metres in length and may weigh over 130 tonnes.

### ▲ WHAT DO WHALES FEED ON?

**Toothed whales, such as dolphins and sperm whales, feed on fish and other large sea animals. Baleen, or whalebone, whales feed on tiny shrimp-like animals.**

Most dolphins feed on fish, squid and cuttlefish near the surface of the sea. Killer whales feed on seals and dolphins as well as fish. Sperm whales dive deep down to feed on squid.

Despite their size, baleen whales, such as the blue whale, humpback whale, minke whale and right whales, are gentle creatures. They feed on plankton, especially the tiny shrimp-like animals called krill.

Instead of teeth, a baleen whale has a number of horny (whalebone) plates on each side of its upper jaw. These form two huge sieves. The whale takes a mouthful of water and krill and closes its mouth. It then forces the water out through the plates, leaving the krill behind.

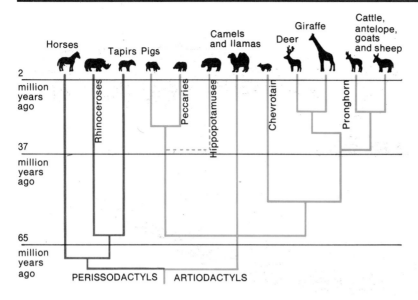

Horses | Tapirs | Pigs | Camels and llamas | Deer | Giraffe | Cattle, antelope, goats and sheep

2 million years ago

Rhinoceroses | Peccaries | Hippopotamuses | Chevrotain | Pronghorn

37 million years ago

65 million years ago

PERISSODACTYLS | ARTIODACTYLS

## ▲ WHAT ARE HOOVED ANIMALS?

**Many plant-eating mammals walk on the tips of toes that have enlarged nails, or hooves. They are often very fast runners.**

## ▼ WHICH ANIMALS ARE RELATED TO HORSES?

**Horses belong to the mammal order Perissodactyla, or odd-toed ungulates. Rhinoceroses and tapirs are the other members of the order.**

The ungulates, or hooved mammals, belong to two separate mammal orders. The perissodactyls have an odd number of toes on each foot. The artiodactyls have an even number of toes on each foot.

Perissodactyls include the

There is only one genus of horses *(Equus)*, of which there are seven living species. Most of the horses we see are breeds of domestic horse. They are all thought to be descended from a wild species known as the tarpan, which became extinct in the 1850s. The only

horses, which walk on just one toe. Ancestors of modern horses had three toes on each foot, but most of the weight was placed on the central toe. Gradually, their descendants lost the use of the two outside toes. The central toe, with its large 'nail', became a single hoof.

Except for hippopotamuses, which have four-toed feet, modern artiodactyls have two toes and are often referred to as cloven-hooved animals. Cloven hooves provide a better grip on slippery rocks, which is why so many artiodactyls are successful mountain-dwellers.

The artiodactyls are a much larger group than the perissodactyls. There are nine families, the largest of which are the deer family and the enormous cattle family.

living wild species of horse is Przewalski's horse of Mongolia.

Other members of the horse family include the three species of zebra in Africa and the two wild asses of Africa and Asia. A donkey is a domesticated breed of African wild ass.

Rhinoceroses are three-toed perissodactyls with horns and tough, armour-like hides. There are five species. The white and black rhinoceroses are both found in Africa. They have two horns and are hairless. The three Asian species (Indian, Javan and Sumatran) have only one horn and have a sparse covering of hair.

Tapirs have four toes on their front feet and three toes on their hind feet. One species lives in south-east Asia. Three species live in South and Central America.

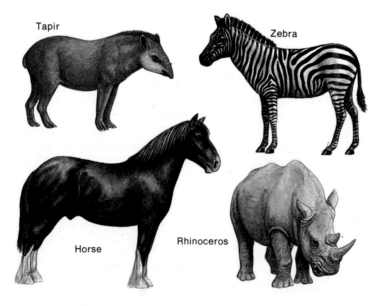

Tapir

Zebra

Horse

Rhinoceros

## ▶ WHICH ANIMALS HAVE HORNS?

**Animals with horns include the giraffe and the okapi, members of the deer family, the pronghorn, and all cattle, antelopes, sheep and goats.**

The four families of horned artiodactyls are different because of the structure of their horns.

The giraffe and okapi have simple, bony knobs covered with hair. The bony horns of deer are known as antlers and a new set grows each year. Except in reindeer, only male deer grow antlers.

Animals belonging to the huge cattle family have permanent horns that consist of a bony cone covered with a horny sheath. Often both males and females have horns.

The cattle family includes antelopes, sheep (such as the mouflon) and goats as well as bison and buffalo.

The pronghorn is the last survivor of a once large family. It sheds the horny sheaths of its horns each year.

Mouflon
Roe deer
Bison

## ◀ HOW MANY KINDS OF ELEPHANT ARE THERE?

**The two species of elephant in the world today are the African and the Asiatic, or Indian, elephant.**

Elephants are the largest living land animals and the larger of the two species is the African elephant. It can grow to a height of about three and a half metres at the shoulder and may weigh over six tonnes.

The African elephant has a less prominent, more rounded forehead than the Asiatic elephant. Its ears and tusks are larger and it has a hollow back.

An elephant's trunk is really the nose and upper lip joined together. It is a long, flexible tube which the elephant uses for carrying food and water to its mouth, dust-bathing and smelling the air.

An elephant's tusks are actually overgrown incisor teeth. They are used as weapons and for digging for water in times of drought.

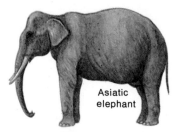
Asiatic elephant

African elephant

## ▶ WHAT IS A HIPPOPOTAMUS?

**The hippopotamus is a distant relative of the pigs and peccaries.**

The name *hippopotamus* means 'river horse'. It is a land animal, but it spends most of its time in water.

During the day it lies partly or almost totally submerged in a slow-moving river. Its eyes and ears are placed near the top of its head, so that as much of its body as possible can remain underwater. And it can close its nostrils when fully submerged.

At night hippopotamuses leave the river and follow well-worn paths to their feeding grounds. They eat grass and, like other herbivores (plant eaters), they chew it up with large grinding teeth. But hippopotamuses also have huge incisors and long, tusk-like canine teeth. Males use these for fighting.

The hippopotamus is found only in Africa. Its smaller relative, the pygmy hippopotamus, is only found in a small part of western Africa.

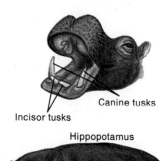
Canine tusks
Incisor tusks
Hippopotamus

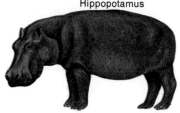

## ▶ WHAT KINDS OF JOINT ARE THERE?

**There are four main kinds of movable joint. They are ball and socket joints, hinge joints, pivot joints and sliding joints.**

Ball and socket joints are found in such places as the shoulders and hips. In this type of joint the head of a long bone fits into a socket on another bone.

Elbows and knees are hinge joints, which act like the hinge on a door. Sliding joints are found in such places as the hands and feet. A pivot joint between the first and second neck vertebrae allows the head to swivel from side to side.

Every joint is surrounded by a tough, fibrous capsule lined with a membrane. This contains a fluid that keeps the joint lubricated.

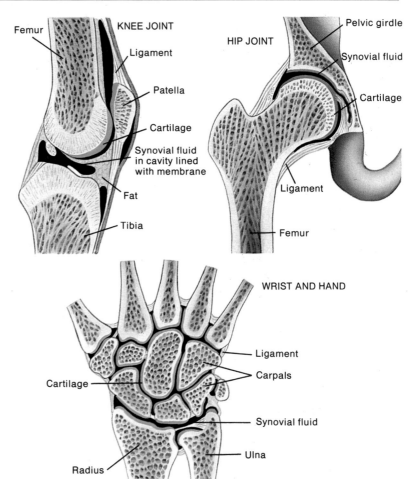

KNEE JOINT
Femur
Ligament
Patella
Cartilage
Synovial fluid in cavity lined with membrane
Fat
Tibia

HIP JOINT
Pelvic girdle
Synovial fluid
Cartilage
Ligament
Femur

WRIST AND HAND
Ligament
Carpals
Cartilage
Synovial fluid
Ulna
Radius

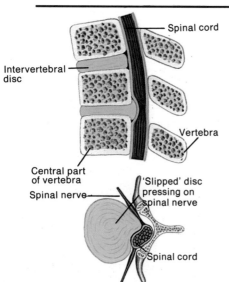

Spinal cord
Intervertebral disc
Vertebra
Central part of vertebra
Spinal nerve
'Slipped' disc pressing on spinal nerve
Spinal cord

## ◀ WHAT IS A SLIPPED DISC?

**A so-called 'slipped disc' is a weakened cartilage in the spine that has bulged out from between its two vertebrae. It may press on a nerve and cause pain.**

An intervertebral disc is a flexible pad consisting of a jelly-like core surrounded by a fibrous cover. It lies directly in between two vertebrae and acts as a shock absorber.

The weakest part of a disc is near the back. Sometimes the fibrous cover develops a crack and the jelly-like material inside bulges out. This is usually caused by putting too much strain on the back.

If the bulge is to one side, it may press on a nerve branching off the spinal cord. In this case the person will feel pain in the area supplied by the nerve, such as the leg or arm. If the bulge pushes straight back into the spinal cord itself, the person may feel pain in such places as the back, neck or chest.

## ▼ WHAT DOES THE SKELETON CONSIST OF?

**The human skeleton is made up of 206 bones.**

The central supporting part of the skeleton is the spine, or vertebral column. This consists of 33 vertebrae.

Seven neck vertebrae support the skull, which is made up of several bones fused together. Below the neck are 12 thoracic vertebrae, which have curved projections known as ribs. All but two of these on each side are also joined to the breast-bone, or sternum. The sternum is fused to the collar bone, or clavicle. This links up with the shoulder bone, or scapula, which is linked to the arm bones.

Below the thoracic vertebrae are five large lumbar vertebrae. At the base of the spine are five fused vertebrae that form the sacrum. Four more fused vertebrae form the coccyx. The sacrum is fused to the bones of the hip girdle, to which are linked the leg bones.

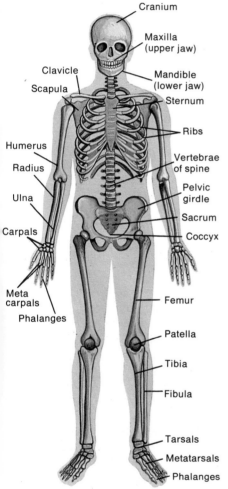

Cranium
Maxilla (upper jaw)
Clavicle
Scapula
Mandible (lower jaw)
Sternum
Ribs
Humerus
Vertebrae of spine
Radius
Pelvic girdle
Ulna
Sacrum
Carpals
Coccyx
Meta carpals
Phalanges
Femur
Patella
Tibia
Fibula
Tarsals
Metatarsals
Phalanges

## ◀ WHAT IS CARTILAGE?

**Cartilage is a glass-like material, often called gristle. It helps to reduce friction and jarring between bones.**

Cartilage is a protein fibre material. It is found in several parts of the body, such as the outer part (pinna) of the ear, the tip of the nose, the larynx and windpipe (trachea).

Cartilage is found in all movable joints, where it helps to reduce friction and acts as a shock absorber. It also makes up the discs between the vertebrae of the spine.

Cartilage has no blood supply and, unlike bone, does not repair itself when damaged. So a damaged knee cartilage may have to be removed by surgery. Sometimes cartilage becomes weakened. Arthritis is partly caused by wearing away of cartilage in joints.

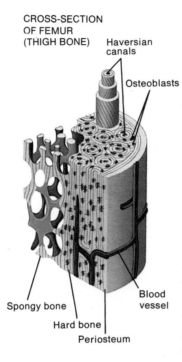

CROSS-SECTION OF FEMUR (THIGH BONE)
Haversian canals
Osteoblasts
Blood vessel
Spongy bone
Hard bone
Periosteum

## ▲ WHAT IS BONE?

**Bone is the hard material from which the parts of the skeleton are made.**

A typical long bone, such as the femur, consists of a long shaft with swellings at each end. The outer part of the bone is made of hard bone and this surrounds a core of spongy bone containing air spaces. Down the middle of the shaft is a cavity, filled with a soft material known as marrow.

The outside of the bone is covered with a fibrous sheath (the periosteum), which is well supplied with blood vessels. Hard bone is made up of a number of long columns. Each one has a channel (Haversian canal) down the middle. This contains blood vessels and is surrounded by several rings of bone cells (osteoblasts), which produce the hard bone material.

Bone consists mostly of calcium, phosphorus and other minerals, which give it great strength. Bone can also be stretched. Elasticity is provided by protein fibres.

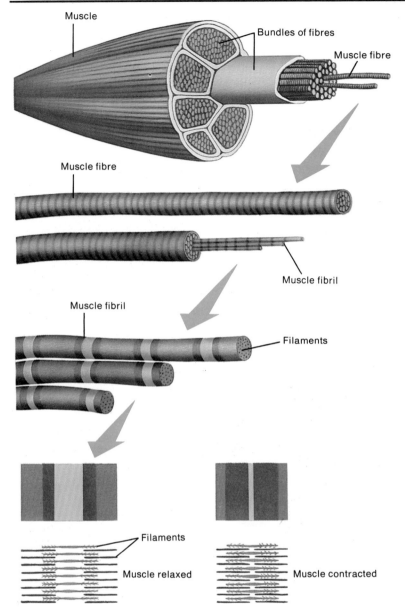

Muscle

Bundles of fibres

Muscle fibre

Muscle fibre

Muscle fibre

Muscle fibril

Muscle fibril

Filaments

Filaments

Muscle relaxed

Muscle contracted

**Muscle is a living tissue that is able to contract. Many of the body's muscles are linked to the bones of the skeleton. Contraction of these muscles gives movement.**

There are three types of muscle. Muscles that move bones are composed of a tissue known as striped muscle. Each major muscle consists of several bundles. Each of these is made up of a number of fibres. Each fibre consists of tiny fibrils.

Muscle fibrils have a striped appearance, which gives this type of muscle its name. The stripes are due to the presence of filaments inside the fibrils. Where filaments overlap, the fibril appears darker. The dark regions of all the fibrils in a fibre coincide. Thus the whole fibre appears to have dark stripes across it.

Muscle contraction is stimulated by nerve impulses. These cause chemical changes in the fibrils. The filaments slide over each other and the whole muscle contracts.

The second type of muscle is called smooth muscle. This consists of long cells, tapered at both ends. The action of smooth muscle is not controlled consciously. It is automatically controlled by a special part of the nervous system. Smooth muscle is found in such places as the lining of the gut and the walls of arteries.

Cardiac muscle is found only in the heart. Its structure is somewhere between that of striped muscle and smooth muscle. It can contract regularly without being stimulated by nerve impulses.

## ▲ WHAT CAUSES CRAMP?

**Cramp is a painful spasm (continuous contraction) of a muscle. It is often caused by lack of oxygen in the muscle.**

When a muscle contracts, it uses up energy. This is provided by respiration – the breakdown of sugar using oxygen with the release of carbon dioxide, water and energy.

During normal exercise the body can take in sufficient oxygen. But after a period of violent exercise the supply of oxygen may start to run out. At this point energy is supplied to the muscle by breaking down the sugar into a chemical called lactic acid. A certain amount of lactic acid can be tolerated. But if too much builds up in the muscle it causes cramp. When the exercise stops, the lactic acid diffuses out of the muscle and is broken down.

Cramp may also be caused by poor blood circulation and by swimming in cold water too soon after a meal.

## ▼ WHAT IS A GLAND?

**A gland produces a chemical substance that is then delivered to a place outside the gland.**

There are two kinds of gland. Exocrine glands have ducts leading to the outside. Sweat glands, for example, are exocrine glands that deliver sweat through coiled ducts to the surface of the skin. Digestive glands in the stomach and intestines produce digestive juices. Salivary glands produce saliva and tear glands produce the fluid that keeps the eyes moist. The liver, which is the largest gland in the body, produces bile.

Endocrine glands, or ductless glands, produce hormones. These are released directly into the bloodstream and are used to control such things as growth and reproduction. One of the most important endocrine glands is the pituitary gland, which is situated in the brain and is about the size of a pea. It produces at least nine hormones.

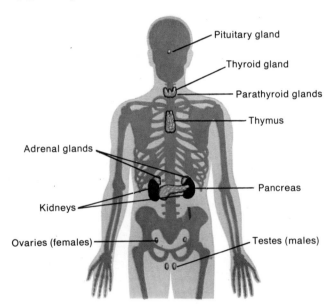

Pituitary gland
Thyroid gland
Parathyroid glands
Thymus
Adrenal glands
Pancreas
Kidneys
Ovaries (females)
Testes (males)

## ▲ WHAT IS A HORMONE?

**A hormone is a chemical produced in one part of the body and transported in the blood to other parts.**

Each hormone has an important controlling effect on the functions of a particular part of the body.

For example, the islets of Langerhans produce the hormone insulin. This controls, via the liver, the level of blood sugar in the body.

The thyroid gland produces thyroxine, which controls the rate at which chemical processes take place in the body. This gland is under the control of the pituitary gland, as are the testes and ovaries.

In males the testes produce testosterone, which controls the development of the sex organs and other male characteristics. In females the ovaries produce oestrogen, which controls female characteristics, and progesterone, which controls pregnancy.

## ▼ WHAT ARE TENDONS AND LIGAMENTS?

**Tendons connect muscles to bones. Ligaments link the bones of a joint.**

Muscles are not directly connected to bones. Instead, each end of a muscle has one or more tendons.

Some tendons are short and thick, such as the two tendons that connect the biceps muscle to the shoulder blade. Some, such as the tendons of the hand and fingers, are long and thin. They extend from the muscles in the forearm into the fingers.

Tendons can sometimes be stretched, particularly when being used in energetic sports. A sprinter, for example, may tear the Achilles tendon in the back of a heel.

A ligament is a flexible band of elastic tissue that links two bones in a joint. Ligaments cannot be stretched and a joint should not be moved beyond the point at which the ligaments are taut. If the joint is moved beyond this point, the ligament tears and the result is a sprain.

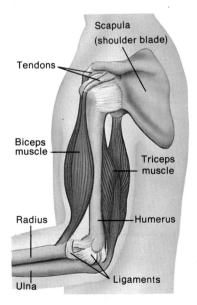

Scapula (shoulder blade)
Tendons
Biceps muscle
Triceps muscle
Radius
Humerus
Ulna
Ligaments

### ▼ WHAT DOES YOUR BRAIN CONSIST OF?

**The brain is a mass of nerve cells and nerve fibres. Different parts of the brain have different functions.**

The largest part of the human brain is the cerebrum, which consists of two cerebral hemispheres. The outer layer of each hemisphere is known as the cerebral cortex. This consists of a much-folded mass of grey matter containing 2500 million nerve cells. Many activities are controlled by this part of the brain, including voluntary, or conscious, movement, speech, hearing, sight, smell, thought and memory. These activities are each controlled by a particular part of the cortex.

Inside the cortex, the rest of the cerebral hemisphere consists of white matter, which is largely made up of nerve fibres.

Other parts of the brain have their own important functions. The corpus callosum is a band of nerve fibres that links the two cerebral hemispheres. The cerebellum helps coordinate movement and control balance. The thalamus is a relay station. It processes all sensory nerve impulses before passing them on to the cortex. The hypothalamus controls body temperature, blood pressure and the pituitary gland. The hind brain, which consists of the medulla oblongata, the pons and the cerebellum, controls the heart, lungs and digestive system.

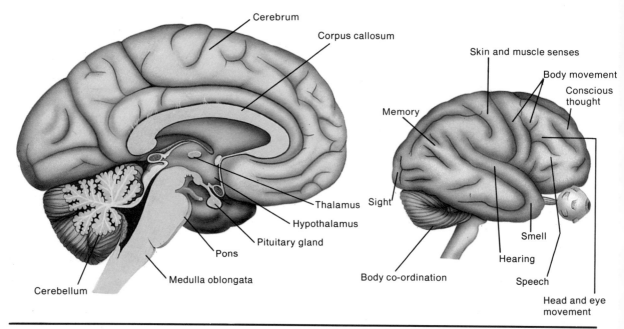

Cerebrum — Corpus callosum — Skin and muscle senses — Body movement — Conscious thought — Memory — Sight — Thalamus — Hypothalamus — Pituitary gland — Pons — Medulla oblongata — Cerebellum — Body co-ordination — Smell — Hearing — Speech — Head and eye movement

### ▶ WHAT IS YOUR 'FUNNY BONE'?

**Your 'funny bone' is a place on the elbow where a nerve passes close to the surface. A sharp knock stimulates this nerve and the brain registers pain.**

There is nothing funny about being struck on the 'funny bone'. This part of the elbow may have been given its name because people thought that it had something to do with the humerus, the bone of the upper arm. But, in fact, the humerus is not involved at all. The 'funny bone' is the knob on the back of the ulna of the forearm.

Most nerves lie well-protected in layers of muscle. However, the ulnar nerve, which runs from the hand to the spinal cord, passes over the elbow just underneath the skin. If it is struck sharply, a stream of impulses is sent to the spinal cord and the brain registers a sharp pain in the elbow. The effect may also be felt in the fingers as tingling.

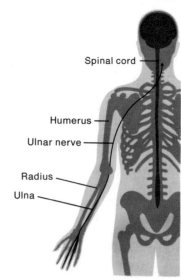

Spinal cord — Humerus — Ulnar nerve — Radius — Ulna

## ▼ WHAT ARE TOUCH AND PAIN?

**The skin contains many sense organs sensitive to touch, pressure, pain, cold and heat. The information they send tells the brain what is happening at any point on the skin.**

Pressure receptors (1) are buried deep in the skin. Touch receptors (2) are nearer the surface, as are cold (3) and heat (4) receptors. Pain receptors are simply free nerve endings (5). Some areas of skin have more sense organs than others. Touch receptors, for example, are plentiful in the fingertips, the tip of the nose and the lips.

Touching an object involves stimulating more than one type of receptor. For example, holding a glass of water involves the sensations of touch, pressure and cold. But holding a glass of water does not stimulate pain receptors. These require more extreme pressures or temperatures before they are stimulated into sending signals to the brain.

## ◄ WHAT IS A REFLEX ACTION?

**A reflex action is one that happens without the person thinking about it.**

When you reach out to pick something up, your brain is sending out a stream of instructions to your muscles. But in a reflex action the brain is not directly involved.

If you place your finger too near a lighted candle, the pain receptors in that finger send out a rapid stream of impulses, which travel to the spinal cord. From there some impulses are relayed to the brain. But before the brain can respond, impulses are sent directly from the spinal cord to your arm and shoulder muscles. These contract and you pull your hand rapidly away from the flame. Reflex actions of this kind help to protect the body from harm.

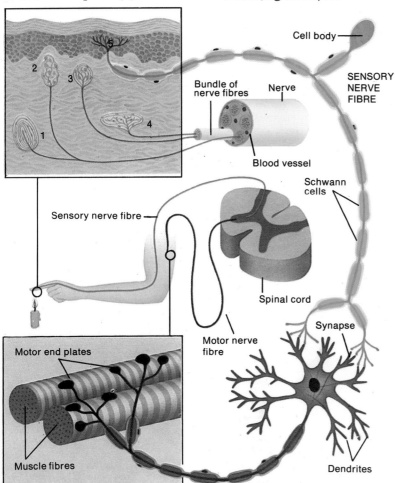

Cell body

Bundle of nerve fibres — Nerve

SENSORY NERVE FIBRE

Blood vessel

Schwann cells

Sensory nerve fibre

Spinal cord

Synapse

Motor nerve fibre

Motor end plates

Muscle fibres

Dendrites

MOTOR NERVE FIBRE

## ▲ WHAT ARE NERVES?

**A nerve consists of bundles of special cells that carry electrical impulses.**

A nerve contains several bundles of nerve fibres, together with some blood vessels. Each fibre, or neuron. is a long cell.

Nerve impulses travel down one or more long fibres called axons. An axon is covered with a sheath (myelin sheath) produced by special cells (Schwann cells). At the tip of an axon are fine fibrils. These connect up with the next neuron by means of a junction called a synapse.

There are two main kinds of neuron. A sensory neuron carries impulses from a sense organ to the spinal cord or brain. A motor neuron carries impulses from the brain or spinal cord to an effector organ, such as a muscle.

Motor neurons have small fibres called dendrites extending from their cell bodies. They connect up to muscle fibres by means of motor end plates.

▼ WHAT ARE ARTERIES AND VEINS?

**Arteries and veins are the main blood vessels of the body. Arteries carry blood from the heart to the tissues. Veins carry blood back to the heart.**

Arteries and veins form a network of tubes around the body. Small blood vessels are known as arterioles and venules. The smallest vessels are called capillaries.

Arteries and veins have three-layered walls. On the inside is a layer of lining cells. Around this is a layer of smooth muscle. On the outside is connective tissue.

Arteries have thicker, more muscular walls than veins.

They carry a fast-flowing stream of blood under pressure from the heart.

Veins are generally larger and more branched than arteries. They carry a slow-moving stream of blood, which is under much less pressure than arterial blood. Veins have one-way valves to prevent the blood flowing backwards.

◀ WHAT IS BLOOD PRESSURE?

**Blood pressure, as measured by a doctor, is the pressure of blood in a main artery.**

Blood pressure is measured by an instrument called a sphygmomanometer. There are two measurements. The first is when the heart is contracting (the systolic pressure) and the other, much lower, pressure is when the heart is resting (diastolic pressure). The results are shown in millimetres of mercury. The average blood pressure of a young person is 120/80.

Blood pressure tends to increase with age and during exercise. Abnormally high blood pressure, or hypertension, may be due to disease, but there is often no easily recognizable cause. Hypertension may strain the heart or damage the kidneys.

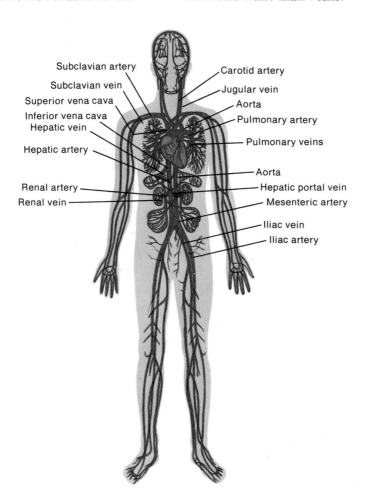

Subclavian artery
Subclavian vein
Superior vena cava
Inferior vena cava
Hepatic vein
Hepatic artery
Renal artery
Renal vein

Carotid artery
Jugular vein
Aorta
Pulmonary artery
Pulmonary veins
Aorta
Hepatic portal vein
Mesenteric artery
Iliac vein
Iliac artery

▲ HOW DOES BLOOD CIRCULATE ROUND YOUR BODY?

**The human body contains between eight and nine pints of blood. The heart pumps it round the body in less than a minute.**

Blood from the body enters the right auricle of the heart through the two main veins (vena cavae). It leaves the heart from the right ventricle and passes, via the pulmonary arteries, to the lungs. There it receives oxygen. It returns back to the left auricle of the heart via the pulmonary veins.

The left ventricle then pumps the blood out through the aorta. Branches from this supply the rest of the body.

When the blood has passed through the tissues, it is collected up by the veins. All but one of the large veins return blood directly to the heart through the vena cavae. The exception is the hepatic portal vein. This collects blood from the intestine and carries it to the liver, which deals with the products of digestion.

### ▶ WHAT IS A BLOOD TRANSFUSION?

**A blood transfusion is the injection of blood from one person (the donor, seen here) into the blood system of another person.**

A blood transfusion may be given to a person with poor blood or one who has lost a lot of blood after an accident.

Usually, blood is supplied from a blood bank. This is a place where blood is stored after being collected from donors.

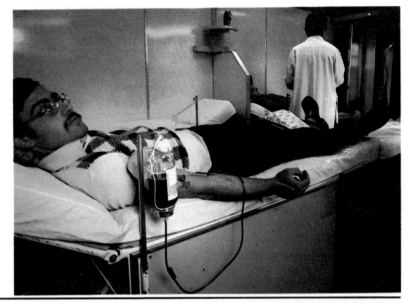

### ▶ WHAT ARE BLOOD GROUPS?

**There are four main groups of blood, known as A, B, AB and O, which contain different factors. If the wrong factors are mixed then blood will clot.**

A person's blood may contain two important types of factor. On the surface of the red blood cells there may be factors known as antigens, of which there are two kinds, A and B. Some people have only antigen-A and are therefore said to have blood group A. Other people have only antigen-B (blood group B). Others have both A and B antigens (blood group AB) and yet others have neither antigen (blood group O).

There may also be antibodies in the serum of the blood. Again there are two types – antibody-a and antibody-b. Antibody-a attacks antigen-A, causing damage to the red blood cells that may make them clump together. Similarly, antibody-b attacks antigen-B. So these antigens and antibodies do not occur in the same blood.

|  | | BLOOD | RECEIVERS | |
|---|---|---|---|---|
| BLOOD DONORS | A (b) | B (a) | AB (—) | 0 (ab) |
| A | | X | | X |
| B | X | | | X |
| AB | X | X | | X |
| 0 | | | | |

 No clumping (can be mixed)

X Clumping of red blood cells (donor and receiver blood must not be mixed)

However, group A blood may contain antibody-b and group B blood may contain antibody-a. Group AB blood contains neither and group O blood may contain both.

In theory, therefore, group A blood should never be mixed with group B or group AB. However, in practice the serum of a group A donor is rapidly diluted in the blood of a group AB receiver. As a result the donor's antibody-b does not have much effect on the antigen-B of the receiver.

For the same reason a person with group AB blood can receive group B blood. A person with group AB blood can therefore receive blood from any donor.

Group AB blood can only be given to a group AB receiver. In all other cases the antigens (A and B) would be attacked by the receiver's antibodies. Group O blood contains no antigens and can be given to anybody. But because group O blood contains both a and b antibodies, a group O person can only receive group O blood.

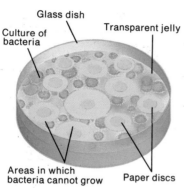

Lid of glass dish

Glass dish

Culture of bacteria

Transparent jelly

Areas in which bacteria cannot grow

Paper discs

## ▲ WHAT IS AN ANTIBIOTIC?

**An antibiotic is a drug that kills bacteria. Many antibiotics are produced from living organisms, such as fungi. There are also man-made types.**

Penicillin was discovered in 1929 and was first used in 1941. Since then many other antibiotics have been discovered, some of which are man-made, or synthetic. Modern antibiotics include streptomycin, chloramphecol, ampicillin, and the tetracyclines.

Some antibiotics can cause harm if taken over a long period of time. One of the safest is still penicillin. However, the use of antibiotics has resulted in new, resistant strains of bacteria.

The illustration shows a number of antibiotics being tested for effectiveness against a particular bacterium. The paper discs are impregnated with the antibiotics. Each one is therefore surrounded by an area in which the colony of bacteria cannot grow. Those with the largest clear areas are the most effective.

## ◄ WHAT ARE GERMS?

**A germ is a tiny living organism that causes disease.**

The world's smallest living organisms include bacteria and viruses and tiny single-celled animals, or protozoa. Some of these are harmless or even useful. Others cause disease and are sometimes known as germs.

Most protozoa are harmless, but a few, such as the malaria parasite and the dysentery amoeba, are disease-causing organisms.

Harmful bacteria may cause disease themselves or they may produce poisonous waste substances. Bacterial diseases include most kinds of food poisoning, bubonic plague, diphtheria, pneumonia, scarlet fever, typhoid fever, typhus and whooping cough.

There are vast numbers of different viruses. Most cause disease. Colds, chicken pox, influenza, measles, mumps and poliomyelitis are all caused by viruses. Some types of cancer are thought to be caused by virus infection.

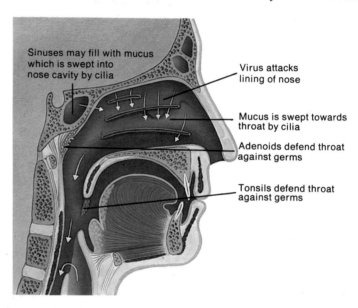

Sinuses may fill with mucus which is swept into nose cavity by cilia

Virus attacks lining of nose

Mucus is swept towards throat by cilia

Adenoids defend throat against germs

Tonsils defend throat against germs

## ▲ WHAT CAUSES A COLD?

**The common cold is a virus disease that affects the linings of the nose, sinuses and, sometimes, the throat and bronchi.**

There are large numbers of viruses that cause colds. A cold begins when infected droplets enter the nose or mouth and a virus attacks the lining of the nose or throat. Between 18 and 48 hours later the lining becomes inflamed and starts to produce mucus, resulting in a running nose.

Mucus is driven by cilia towards the throat. At the back of the throat are the adenoids and tonsils. These are lumps of lymph tissue, whose main task is to defend the throat against infection.

Despite these organs the virus often does enter the throat, which also becomes inflamed and sore. If the bronchi of the lungs become infected the result is a cough. Mucus from the throat and bronchi is driven down the oesophagus to the stomach. In time, the body's natural defences deal with the virus.

▶ WHICH PARTS OF THE
BODY CAN BE REPLACED
WITH ARTIFICIAL PARTS?

## Using modern plastics, metals and other materials, it is now possible to place over 40 artificial parts into the human body.

Modern artificial limbs are very sophisticated and many work almost as well as real limbs. Many other parts can also be replaced. Metal hip joints have eased the lives of many arthritis sufferers. And a number of other bones and joints can be replaced with metal or plastic parts.

Many artificial parts are not essential. Some just improve a person's appearance. But others are important in easing discomfort and pain and some replacement parts save lives. Artificial heart valves, arteries and veins keep the blood system working properly.

In the future some even more vital organs may be replaced. There may be small, self-contained artificial hearts, miniature artificial kidneys, artificial lungs and replacement livers.

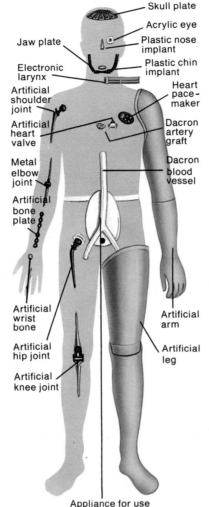

Skull plate
Acrylic eye
Plastic nose implant
Jaw plate
Plastic chin implant
Electronic larynx
Heart pace-maker
Artificial shoulder joint
Dacron artery graft
Artificial heart valve
Metal elbow joint
Dacron blood vessel
Artificial bone plate
Artificial wrist bone
Artificial arm
Artificial hip joint
Artificial leg
Artificial knee joint
Appliance for use after removal of part of small intestine

◀ WHAT IS A PACEMAKER?

## An artificial pacemaker is used when a person's own heart pacemaker is not working properly. It is an electronic device for stimulating the heart.

Heart muscle contracts regularly. However, its natural rate (about 40 beats per minute) is too slow. To increase the rate to around 70 beats, the heart has its own pacemaker. This is a small mass, or node, of nerve tissue in the right auricle.

Certain heart diseases cause this pacemaker to fail. However, the heart can be kept going with a battery-powered electronic pace-maker. Some artificial pacemakers are implanted in the chest. Others are small enough to be passed along a vein to the heart. The simplest pacemakers keep the heart going at a steady 70 beats per minute. But some-times it is possible to get the person's own nervous system to control the pacemaker. In this case the heart can still beat faster or slower according to the body's needs.

▶ WHAT IS TRANSPLANT
SURGERY?

## In a transplant operation a surgeon replaces a damaged or diseased organ with a healthy one.

Surgeons can now transplant several organs of the body. The main problem that occurs is rejection. The natural body defences of the person receiving a new organ may react as though the new organ was an invading germ and attack it.

Some organs, such as bone,

blood vessels, heart valves and corneas (the transparent 'windows' of the eyes) can be transplanted without rejection problems. However, a kidney or a heart has to be well matched with the tissues of the receiver to reduce the chances of rejection. Drugs

that control the body's defence system are also used.

A new kidney or heart is taken from the donor's body within 30 minutes of death. It is then sent rapidly, as shown in the photograph, to the hospital where the receiver is waiting.

# TRANSPORT

### ▼ WHAT IS A CABLE CAR?

**A cable car is a cabin hung from cables slung between towers. It can go up or down a mountain.**

Most cable cars work in pairs in a way that saves some of the power needed to make them

both work. This is called a funicular system.

Each car hangs from a steel suspension cable by means of a metal frame with grooved wheels that rest on the cable.

A haulage cable pulls each car along. This cable is fixed to the cars and looped around a drum at the top of the cableway. An electric motor at the top hauls in cable on one side and pays it out on the other. So as one car rises, the other descends.

Brakes may act on a third cable to stop each car.

### ▼ WHAT ARE THE MAIN PARTS OF A RAILWAY TRACK?

**These are the roadbed, sleepers and two parallel lengths of steel rail.**

The roadbed is a wide, flat firm pathway. It is covered with ballast: a layer of stones or crushed rock. Rain drains away through this ballast.

A row of concrete, steel or wooden beams is laid across the ballast. These sleepers are strong enough to support huge loads. The rails are laid crosswise over the sleepers. Tie-plates between rails and sleepers help to spread the load, and spikes, bolts or clips join rails to sleepers.

Joint bars, or fish-plates, join lengths of rail or these are welded together. Welded rails give trains the smoothest ride.

Rails  Ballast
Sleepers
Spikes
Tie-plate

### ▼ WHICH ROAD VEHICLES RUN ON RAILS?

**These are passenger carriages called trams or streetcars. They run in the streets of many cities.**

A modern tram looks like a small railway carriage. Two

or more carriages are sometimes coupled together. Trams run on rails set in the road, level with its surface. A frame of rods called a pantograph juts up from the tram roof to collect electric current from an overhead wire. This current works the motor that drives the tram.

Trams can move more people more smoothly than buses. Also, if electricity is cheap, they may be cheaper to run. But some prove very costly. Many cities have replaced trams with buses.

54

## ▲ WHAT IS A MONORAIL?

**A monorail is a railway with only one overhead rail. Some monorail trains run along the top of a rail. Other types hang below a rail.**

Monorail cars that rest on the rail keep their balance with the help of a gyroscope, or guide wheels gripping the sides of the rail. Cars slung below the rail have wheels that run on top of it. Split-rail monorails have two rails close together and a roof that keeps them dry.

Many monorail cars run on rubber wheels that help to reduce noise. Power can come from a gas turbine, a petrol engine or an electric motor driven by the current from an electric rail. Monorail cars can be given automatic controls to make them stop and start, and slow down where the track curves.

A monorail track is so narrow that its supports can be just a row of slim columns. So monorails need not take up much space, and can be built over busy streets.

Building and running a monorail costs less than building and running an ordinary railway, and the cars are speedy and safe. They are able to carry people across a city a great deal faster than buses or cars.

## ▼ WHAT IS A HOVERTRAIN?

**Hovertrains are trains that hover over a special kind of rail raised just above the ground. They do not run on rails in the same way as ordinary trains.**

There are two main kinds of hovertrain. One depends on air to keep it up, while the other is held up by magnets. Both fit over and around a track that looks rather like a low concrete wall with a pavement on each side. Both give a very fast, smooth ride.

France's *Aérotrain* produces jets of air which blow so hard that they hold the train just above the track. A gas-turbine aero-engine on the roof gives power, and the *Aérotrain* can easily reach 300 kilometres an hour.

Another kind of hovertrain uses the magnetic levitation method. These trains have built-in magnets that are repelled by magnets in the track they run on. This keeps the trains hovering, while a magnetic force in the track pulls them along at enormous speed. One Japanese research vehicle broke the world speed record by reaching 520 kilometres an hour.

Hovertrains can be fast, quiet and vibration-free. But they need special track that must be unusually straight and level. This is largely why hovertrains are so far mainly just experimental.

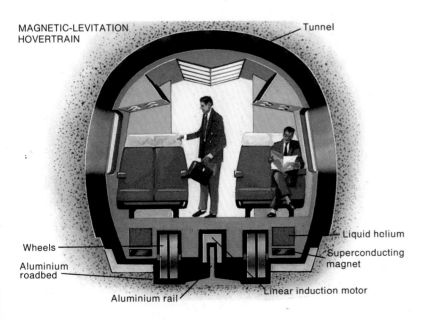

MAGNETIC-LEVITATION HOVERTRAIN

Tunnel

Wheels

Aluminium roadbed

Aluminium rail

Linear induction motor

Liquid holium

Superconducting magnet

## ▲ WHAT IS A SEAPLANE?

**Seaplanes are aircraft that take off and land on water. They are specially designed to remain afloat**

Many seaplanes have light, hollow, streamlined floats fixed below the wings in place of landing wheels. The floats rest on water and make the aircraft buoyant. They also help to stop the seaplane tipping over.

Seaplanes called flying boats have a boat-shaped body that combines the main floats with the fuselage.

Aircraft with retractable wheels built into the floats are called amphibians. These planes can use either land or water as their runway.

Seaplanes need no specially built runway, so they can stop at more places than ordinary aircraft. But they need fairly smooth water.

## ▶ WHAT IS A JUMBO JET?

**Any huge, wide-bodied jet transport plane may be called a jumbo jet. But people use the name for the Boeing 747, the first type of giant jet transport aircraft.**

BOEING 747

BOEING 707

A Boeing 747 is over 70 metres long and it has a wingspan of nearly 60 metres. The cabin is over six metres wide. Four immensely powerful turbofan engines are slung beneath the wings and thrust the aircraft along at up to 969 kilometres an hour. A 747 carries enough fuel to cross an ocean.

Most 747s are airliners. They can carry from 385 to over 500 passengers. But some 747s carry freight. Just one can move more freight in a year than all the world's airliners carried in 1939.

Other giant jets include the Douglas DC10 and the Lockheed Tristar.

## ▶ WHAT ARE THE MAIN CONTROLS ON AN AIRCRAFT?

**A plane has three main controls: a throttle lever, a control column and a rudder bar.**

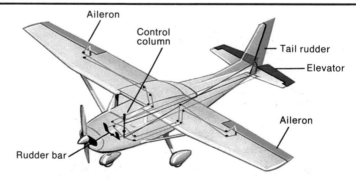

Aileron

Control column

Tail rudder

Elevator

Aileron

Rudder bar

When the pilot moves the throttle lever back and forth he or she alters the engine power and, therefore, the speed.

Pulling the control column back lifts tail flaps called elevators. This makes the plane climb. Pushing the control column forward lowers the elevators and the plane begins to dive.

When the pilot pulls the column to one side, this lifts one aileron (outer wing flap) and lowers the other. This makes the plane bank for a safe turn.

Moving the rudder bar turns the tail rudder left or right. This steers the plane's nose to the left or right.

## ► WHICH IS THE WORLD'S FASTEST AIRCRAFT?

**The holder of the official air speed record since 1976 has been a Lockheed SR-71A, although some aircraft have actually flown much faster.**

The Lockheed SR-71 is a big reconnaissance jet aircraft, flying in the US Air Force. It is made of lightweight titanium alloys and painted black.

The Lockheed SR-71 was built to fly high, fast and far to avoid detection as it spied upon other countries.

In July 1976, an SR-71A broke the official air speed record when it flew over a course in California at 3529.56 kilometres an hour.

Rocket-powered aircraft can do still better. In 1981 the Space Shuttle craft *Columbia* first soared into space at 26,715 kilometres an hour.

## ▲ WHAT IS A GLIDER?

**Gliders are aircraft without engines. They can soar up on rising air and glide down on sinking air as sledges slide downhill.**

Most gliders have long, narrow wings rather like a seagull's. A glider's cockpit contains controls and instruments like many of those in powered planes. But most gliders also have a sensitive variometer. This shows the rate at which air lifts or drops the aircraft.

Like a powered aircraft, a glider can take off only when it is moving. A glider can be launched in several ways. It may be catapulted from a hilltop by an elastic cord, pulled into the air by a line being wound on to a drum, or towed by a car or an engine-driven plane.

Glider pilots soar on air currents rising up ridges and over heated land. They glide in sinking air currents over valleys and lakes.

Wings swept back

Wings open for take-off and landing

## ▲ WHAT IS A SWING-WING AIRCRAFT?

**A swing-wing aircraft is one where the pilots can change the shape of the wings as they fly.**

Changing wing shape has big advantages, for each shape works best only in certain conditions.

On swing-wing planes the wings pivot so they can stick out at the sides or lie back. To take off, a pilot sets them at maximum span. For cruising flight they are partly swept back. For low-level attack or supersonic flight they are folded back against the tail. For landing, the pilot brings the wings forward and out again, and operates flaps and slats to increase their surface area.

Sir Barnes Wallis designed a swing-wing plane in the 1950s. But the first to be built was General Dynamics' F-111. This United States warplane first flew in 1964.

### ▶ WHAT DOES A DREDGER DO?

**Dredgers remove mud, sand or shingle from the beds of rivers, lakes, canals or harbours. This work keeps waterways open and can be a way of gathering building materials and mining tin and gold.**

Exactly what a dredger does depends upon how it is designed.

Bucket dredgers use an endless chain of buckets to scoop up silt. They tip this into a chute that lets it slide down into a barge moored beside the dredger.

Dipper dredgers scoop up material in a huge mechanical shovel that can be swung around and lowered from a boom. Grab dredgers work in a similar way, but use a scoop with jaws that can be closed and opened.

Suction dredgers are like giant vacuum cleaners. Their powerful pumps suck up mud or sand through pipes.

### ▶ WHAT IS A SUPER-TANKER?

**Supertankers are giant oil tankers. They are built to carry huge loads of crude oil from oil-fields around the world to industrial regions such as north-west Europe.**

By the 1980s supertankers included the largest vessels of any kind. Biggest of all was the *Seawise Giant* which can carry a total load of over 560,000 tons. This monster is roughly as long as four soccer pitches laid end to end, and wider than six tennis courts placed side by side. Yet a handful of crew can manage the ship.

People built supertankers because they were cheap to run. It costs less to shift a huge load in one ship than to divide that load among several ships.

But huge size brings some drawbacks. Supertankers cannot stop or turn quickly. If one runs aground its spilt oil pollutes huge areas.

### ▶ WHAT ARE BARGES USED FOR?

**Most barges are flat-bottomed boats used for carrying heavy loads on inland waterways.**

Barges mainly carry building materials like cement, wooden planks and sand. They also carry food, like grain and sugar, or fuels like coal and oil. Some roll-on roll-off barges can take over 300 lorries.

Many barges have no engines of their own. Some are towed by horses or electric engines that run on rails along the banks of rivers or canals. Others are pushed or pulled by tugs. One tug can pull a number of barges at once.

Moving heavy loads by barge may be slower than shifting them by road or rail but it is also less expensive.

The name *barge* is also used to describe a large motorboat carrying a high-ranking naval officer, or an elegantly decorated and roomy pleasure boat.

## ▼ WHAT IS A PADDLE STEAMER?

**In this kind of steamship the engine turns one or more paddle wheels. Each paddle wheel has spokes that end in broad blades. These beat the water and push it backward to thrust the steamer forward.**

Some paddle steamers have two paddle wheels, one at each side. Others have only one paddle wheel fitted to the ship's stern. The side wheels are usually covered by curved paddle boxes that may be decorated.

Many tugs and excursion vessels once had side paddles. These helped the boats to make sharp turns near piers.

In the United States, big stern-wheel paddle steamers once took thousands of passengers up and down the Mississippi River. Such ships had shallow hulls but carried heavy loads.

Most paddle steamers have been replaced by diesel-engine ships with screws instead of paddles.

## ▲ WHAT IS A HYDROFOIL?

**This looks like an ordinary craft until it picks up speed. Then it rises on underwater wings called foils. Hydrofoils are used mostly as ferries making short, fast trips.**

Foils increase a hydrofoil's speed because they reduce the friction caused by the hull rubbing against the water.

Most hydrofoils have one of four main types of foil. Ladder foils are arranged like rungs on a ladder: the faster the vessel moves, the more the foils show up above the surface. Depth-effect foils are single wings that ride just under the surface and work well in calm, shallow water. Submerged foils are small foils that ride deeper down at angles that can be controlled. They work well in rough seas.

Most modern hydrofoils have surface-piercing foils. These are shaped like a shallow V and they keep the craft stable as it turns sharply or speeds through steep waves.

## ▲ WHAT IS A SUBMERSIBLE USED FOR?

**These small, powered craft are designed for underwater work or exploration.**

Since the 1950s inventors have developed many kinds of submersible.

The first to be produced was the French *Soucoupe*, or diving saucer. Its crew could study sea-bed life to a depth of 300 metres.

Later came the *Aluminaut*. This American submersible's crew of three could operate grappling arms to rescue sunken objects lying as much as 4600 metres deep.

Nowadays manned and robot submersibles do valuable work on undersea oil and gas pipes and other installations.

Some unmanned submersibles have built-in cameras, sonar equipment, power tools and lights. An observer and a pilot at the surface can guide this type of submersible by remote control as it works 600 metres below.

### ▲ WHAT IS A STOCK-CAR RACE?

**This is a race between cars of standard models, not racing models or sports cars. They race around an oval track.**

Stock cars may look like ordinary passenger cars, but they tend to have 'souped up' engines and improved brakes and suspension. Also they are often specially strengthened. In the United States they roar around banked tracks at over 300 kilometres an hour.

### ▼ WHAT IS A ROTARY ENGINE?

**A rotary engine is an internal combustion engine. It has a revolving rotor which turns a drive shaft.**

The most-used kind of rotary engine is the Wankel engine. This has a rotor inside a chamber. The rotor looks like a triangle with bulging sides. The tips touch the wall of the chamber, but there are gaps between its sides and the chamber wall.

The rotor keeps turning fast instead of slowing and speeding up like a piston, and it needs no crankshaft to turn to-and-fro motion into round-and-round motion.

As the rotor turns, it opens and shuts two openings in the chamber wall. One lets a fuel-air mixture enter a gap between the rotor and chamber. The rotor compresses this mixture. A spark plug makes it explode, and forces the rotor to keep turning. Burnt gases escape from a second opening in the chamber wall.

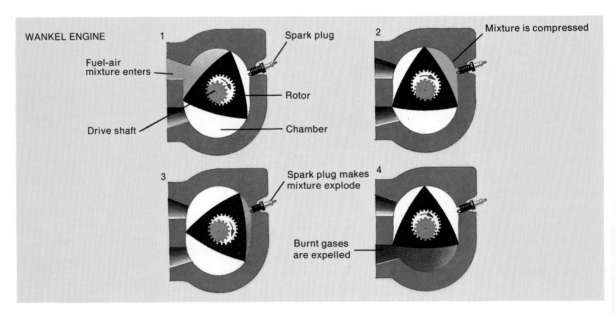

WANKEL ENGINE
1 Spark plug
Fuel-air mixture enters
Rotor
Drive shaft
Chamber

2 Mixture is compressed

3 Spark plug makes mixture explode
Burnt gases are expelled

4

## ▶ WHICH IS THE WORLD'S FASTEST CAR?

**When this book was being written, the American *Budweiser Rocket* was the fastest car, but Britain's *Thrust 2* held the land speed record.**

In 1979 the American driver Stan Barrett may have reached 1190.377 kilometres an hour when he drove the *Budweiser Rocket* at Edwards Air Base in California. But timing did not meet the strict conditions laid down for setting a new official world land speed record.

That was still held by another rocket-powered car, Gary Gabelich's *Blue Flame*. In 1970, this reached a speed of 1001.473 kilometres an hour on the Bonneville Salt Flats in Utah. *Blue Flame's* record stood until 1983. Then Britain's Richard Noble reached 1019.471 kilometres an hour in jet-powered *Thrust 2*, also in America. These cars resembled aircraft fuselages.

## ▶ WHAT IS AN ELECTRIC CAR?

**An electric car is powered by electricity stored in heavy, powerful batteries.**

In an electric car the energy stored in the batteries operates an electric motor that turns the wheels.

An electric car is quieter than a petrol-driven car and it gives off no unpleasant exhaust gases. To recharge its batteries you just plug the car into a mains electricity supply, as you plug in a record player.

But most electric cars that have been built have disadvantages. They cannot travel very fast. Their batteries are so heavy that just moving them wastes energy. Also, electric cars cannot travel very far before their batteries run down.

Electric cars are still only experimental. But if petrol should become very scarce and costly many may be built as useful city runabouts.

## ▶ WHAT IS A ROAD TRAIN?

**This is the name given to a large, powerful truck and the several trailers it tows behind it.**

Road trains are used for carrying huge loads over long distances. This can be the cheapest way of shifting heavy, bulky cargoes across countryside which has no railways, rivers or canals.

Only broad highways with gentle curves are suitable for taking road trains. Each is so long that no car could overtake safely on a narrow, winding road. Indeed, Australia forbids road trains on many normal highways. The drivers must use dirt tracks instead. Special tyres enable them to travel safely over loose, uneven surfaces at speeds of up to 90 kilometres an hour.

Driving for thousands of kilometres is lonely work. It can be dangerous, too, if a truck breaks down in a hot desert or an Arctic blizzard.

# SCIENCE

**Everything is made of tiny particles called atoms. Every atom is made of even smaller particles. In the centre is the nucleus. Around it move very tiny particles called electrons.**

An atom is about a hundred-millionth of a centimetre across, and it is mostly empty space! The nucleus is 10,000 times smaller than the atom, and the electrons are ten times smaller still.

The electrons move in orbits in the space around the nucleus. The nucleus is made of small particles called protons and neutrons. The simplest atom is a hydrogen atom. It contains one electron moving around a nucleus of one proton. The biggest normal atom is a uranium atom. It has 92 electrons and its nucleus is made of 92 protons and 146 neutrons.

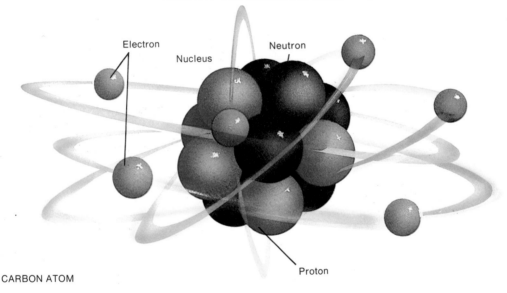

Electron

Nucleus

Neutron

Proton

CARBON ATOM

▲ WHAT IS AN ELECTRON?

**An electron is a very tiny piece of electricity. The amount of electricity that an electron has is the smallest amount that it is possible to have.**

When an electric current flows through a wire, electrons leave the atoms in the wire and move to other atoms. To light a torch bulb, more than a million million million electrons have to flow through the wire in the bulb every second.

The electrons that move around the nucleus of an atom give it a kind of electrical shell.

The electrons each have a negative electric charge. This electric charge produces an electric field, and the field repels other negative electric fields. If one atom approaches another, the electric fields around their electron shells repel each other and prevent them from touching.

The protons in the nucleus of an atom each have a positive electric charge. Normally, an atom has the same number of electrons and protons. The neutrons have no charge. The electrons' negative charges balance the protons' positive charges, so that the atom has no electric charge as a whole.

Atoms can easily lose or gain electrons, but not protons or neutrons, which are protected by the electron shells around the nucleus. The atoms of the substances in batteries have gained or lost electrons. The battery makes electrons flow through the wires connected to it to bring its atoms back to normal.

## ▼ WHAT IS A MOLECULE?

**Almost everything is made of molecules. Molecules are tiny particles that are too small to be seen except in the most powerful microscopes. A molecule is in fact a group of atoms.**

**In a pure substance like pure water, every molecule is made of the same number of the same atoms. Each water molecule has two hydrogen atoms and one oxygen atom.**

In molecules, the atoms are linked by bonds. These bonds are electrical forces that hold the atoms close but not touching one another. The bonds form by an exchange of electrons between the atoms in the molecule.

A molecule may have as few as two atoms. The oxygen gas in the air consists of oxygen molecules each containing two oxygen atoms. Some substances are made of molecules containing thousands of atoms in chains or complex shapes.

## ▼ WHAT IS A COMPOUND?

**A compound is a substance in which the molecules are made of atoms of different elements. Water is a compound because its molecules contain hydrogen and oxygen atoms. It is a compound of hydrogen and oxygen. It is not the same as a mixture of hydrogen and oxygen. In such a mixture, there are separate hydrogen molecules and oxygen molecules.**

Compounds include salt, which is a compound of sodium and chlorine, and sugar, which is a compound of carbon, hydrogen and oxygen.

The bonds between the atoms in the molecules of compounds cannot easily be broken. A compound therefore cannot easily be changed into its elements. Electricity is needed to break down water or salt into their elements, for example.

There are many natural compounds, as well as new ones produced by scientists.

## ▲ WHAT IS AN ELEMENT?

**Everything is made of elements. The hydrogen and oxygen in water are both elements. In an element, all the atoms are the same. Other elements include carbon, mercury, chlorine, nitrogen, iron, aluminium, copper, silver and gold. Fewer than 100 different elements exist naturally in the whole universe.**

All the atoms in an element are the same because the nucleus of each atom contains the same number of protons. A carbon atom contains six protons, and this number is called the element's atomic number.

If the number of protons changes, then the element becomes a different element. However, the number of electrons and neutrons in the atom can change slightly without the element changing. The forces that hold the protons in the nucleus are very strong indeed. It takes a lot of energy to change the number of protons.

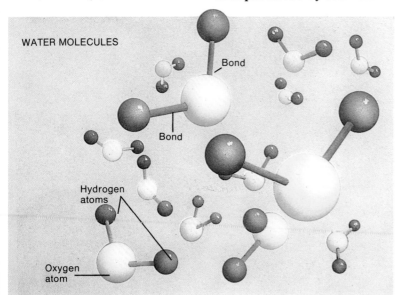

WATER MOLECULES

Bond

Bond

Hydrogen atoms

Oxygen atom

### ▼ WHAT IS A SOLID?

**A solid is a substance or a material that does not flow. Solids include ice, steel, wood, paper, cloth, salt and sugar. A piece of a solid may bend, stretch or contract in size, but it does not otherwise change its shape.**

A solid is made of atoms or molecules that are arranged in rows or patterns. The atoms or molecules are pulled together by forces between them. If the forces are strong,

SOLID

Molecules in rows

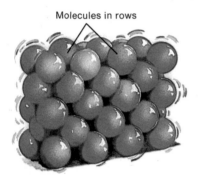

then the solid is hard and tough. If they are weak, then the solid is soft or may break easily.

The atoms or molecules constantly vibrate to and fro over a short distance. The amount of vibration depends on how hot or cold the solid is. The hotter it is, the more they vibrate.

At a certain temperature, the atoms or molecules begin to break away from one another. The solid melts and becomes a liquid. This temperature is called the melting point of the solid.

### ▼ WHAT IS A LIQUID?

**A liquid can flow and change its shape. Liquids include water, milk, mercury, petrol and oil. When a certain amount of liquid is placed in a container, it takes the shape of the container but its volume remains the same.**

In a liquid, the atoms or molecules are in small groups that move about on their own. This is why a liquid can flow and take up any shape, and

LIQUID

Groups of molecules

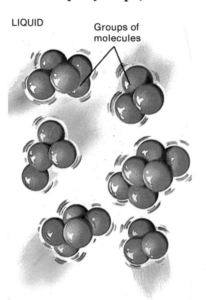

why a piece of a solid can move through a liquid.

As a liquid gets hotter, the groups of atoms or molecules move faster. They begin to break up into single atoms or molecules and leave the liquid. A gas is formed. At the boiling point, the liquid boils and all of it turns into gas.

When a liquid gets colder, the groups of atoms or molecules slow down. At the freezing point, they settle into rows and the liquid becomes a solid. The boiling point of water is 100°C and the freezing point is 0°C.

### ▼ WHAT IS A GAS?

**A gas is a substance that flows and increases in size until it fills a container. The air is a mixture of gases. It has no container and spreads out over the entire world. As well as oxygen and other gases in the air, gases include steam, chlorine, hydrogen and helium.**

In a gas, the atoms or molecules are not linked together. They move about singly in all directions at great

GAS

Single molecules

speed. This is why a gas rapidly takes up all the space in a container and fills it. If there are more atoms or molecules, they are closer together and the pressure of the gas is greater.

As a gas gets colder, its atoms or molecules slow down. At the boiling point, they form groups and the gas condenses to a liquid. Steam condenses to water at 100°C.

A vapour is a form of gas that exists below the boiling point. It forms above a liquid as single atoms or molecules escape from the liquid.

## ▶ WHAT IS WATER MADE OF?

**Water is made of hydrogen and oxygen. In water molecules, hydrogen atoms and oxygen atoms are linked together. They do not normally come apart.**

Water can be changed into hydrogen gas and oxygen gas by passing an electric current through it. In fact, water does not conduct electricity very well, so a little acid is usually added.

In the water molecules, the hydrogen and oxygen atoms are bound together because they have formed a bond with electrons. The electric current causes these electrons to return to the atoms, breaking the bonds in the molecules. Separate hydrogen atoms and oxygen atoms are formed, and they link up to give hydrogen molecules and oxygen molecules. As they do so, bubbles of hydrogen gas and oxygen gas form on the electrodes in the water.

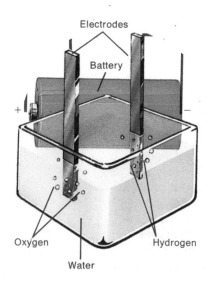

Electrodes

Battery

Oxygen

Hydrogen

Water

---

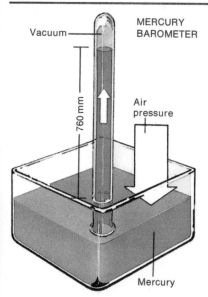

Vacuum

MERCURY BAROMETER

760 mm

Air pressure

Mercury

## ◀ WHAT IS MERCURY?

**Mercury is the only liquid metal. All other metals, like iron, copper or aluminium, are solid. However, mercury becomes solid if it gets cold enough. But it has to be very cold, at least −39°C or colder.**

Mercury is unusual only because its freezing point of −39°C is the lowest of any metal. This is also lower than the normal range of temperature at which we live.

Mercury is therefore a good liquid to use in thermometers. Mercury thermometers can measure temperatures from −39°C up to 356°C, the boiling point of mercury.

Mercury is also used in mercury barometers, which measure the pressure of the atmosphere. The pressure of the air forces mercury to a certain height in a tube with a vacuum at the top. The height depends on the air pressure, which can be measured in millimetres of mercury. Normal atmospheric pressure equals 760mm of mercury.

---

## ▶ WHAT IS AIR MADE OF?

**Air is made of the gases oxygen, nitrogen and argon. The air always contains the same amounts of these gases. Unless the air is dry, it also contains some water vapour.**

The approximate proportions of the gases in pure air at sea-level are nitrogen 78%, oxygen 21% and argon 1%. There are also very small amounts of carbon dioxide, neon and helium.

The air also contains varying amounts of water vapour and gases that come from burning fuel, as well as dust particles floating in the air. The amounts of these gases and dust depend on the location.

In the upper air, above a height of 100 kilometres, there is much less nitrogen and more oxygen.

Life on Earth depends on the oxygen and nitrogen in the air because plants and animals need these elements to grow. Argon has no effect on living things.

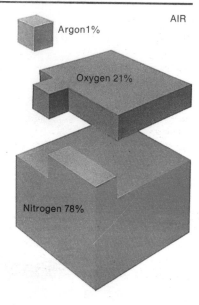

AIR

Argon 1%

Oxygen 21%

Nitrogen 78%

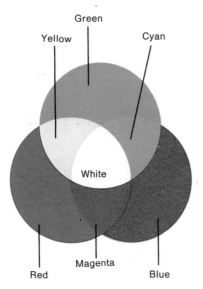

## ▲ WHAT ARE PRIMARY COLOURS?

**All colours can be made by mixing any of three main colours. These are called primary colours. In paints and inks, the three primary colours are yellow, cyan (blue-green) and magenta (red-blue). Mixing yellow and cyan, for example, gives green.**

When coloured lights are mixed together, the three primary colours are red, green and blue. Red and green mix to give yellow; blue and green form cyan; and red and blue make magenta. All three give white.

We can make all colours from just three primary light colours because our eyes are sensitive to red, green and blue. When we see a particular colour, our eyes pick out the amounts of red, green and blue in it and mix them together.

The primary colours in paints and inks are different because they produce colour by reflecting light of a particular colour from a surface.

## ▼ WHAT DOES WHITE LIGHT CONSIST OF?

**White light is in fact a mixture of colours. If you pass white light through a glass prism, it splits up into a band of colours**

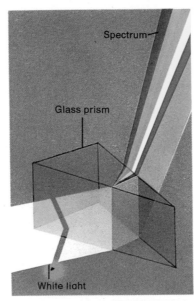

## ▲ WHAT CAUSES A MIRAGE?

**A mirage is an image of a place or a thing that you can see on the ground some distance away. Mirages happen on warm days, and often look like pools of water. You see them because warm air near the ground bends light rays. An image of the sky appears on the ground. This is the 'pool' of water.**

When a mirage forms, light rays from the sky or an object

called a spectrum. If the spectrum colours are passed through another prism, they mix together to give white.

The colours of the spectrum are the same as the colours of the rainbow. This is because the raindrops that form a rainbow each split sunlight up in the same way as a prism.

The pattern is a mixture of three bands of the primary colours, red, green and blue. The other colours form where these three bands overlap and mix together.

A prism and raindrops split up white light because the rays of light bend as they pass into and out of the prism or raindrop. Each colour mixed together in the white light bends by a different amount. Red bends least and violet most.

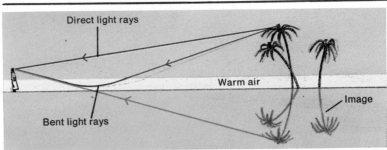

such as a tree bend as they pass through warm air near the ground. This happens because the air gets warmer near the hot ground and light rays bend when they pass between cooler and warmer air.

The tree and sky are seen in their normal positions by light rays that come directly to the eyes. The rays that have been bent also reach the eyes, which assume that they too have come directly. An image of the tree and sky is therefore seen on the ground beneath the tree.

## ▼ WHAT ARE OPTICAL FIBRES?

**Optical fibres are long, thin threads of glass. Light travels along them, no matter how much they bend. Doctors can look inside the body without cutting it open by using optical fibres. The fibres send light into the body, and are attached to tiny lenses so that they can bring pictures back.**

In the future, homes are likely to be connected by cables

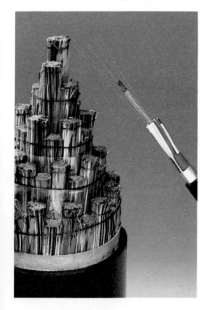

containing optical fibres, just as they are connected by telephone wires now.

Laser beams will travel along the fibres, bringing television pictures to homes and linking computers to homes.

Laser beams can be used to produce signals that contain a lot of information – far more than can be sent by telephone or radio. The optical-fibre cable in the photograph can carry 7680 telephone conversations, compared with 6000 conversations on the old copper cable.

## ▼ WHAT IS A LASER?

**A laser is a machine that produces a very powerful beam of light. The beam is very thin, and it is not like ordinary light. The rays in a laser beam travel in step with one another, rather like soldiers marching in step. Ordinary light rays do not do this.**

Light rays consist of waves of light energy. The energy in the rays rises and falls rather like waves in water but millions of times a second.

In ordinary light, the waves rise and fall at different times. In laser light, the waves rise and fall exactly together, giving laser light much more energy than ordinary light.

Lasers contain a light source such as a flash tube that pumps light into a material like a ruby crystal. Mirrors store the light in the material so that its energy builds up. It is then all released in a sudden burst.

The light waves formed in this way all rise and fall exactly together, and a beam of laser light emerges from the crystal.

## ▼ WHAT ARE LASERS USED FOR?

**Because laser light is so powerful, laser beams can be used to weld metals. Surgeons can use lasers instead of knives in operations. Laser beams can also send information rather as radio waves do, but in huge amounts.**

Because the light waves in a laser beam are all in step and the beam is very straight, lasers can be used to measure distances very accurately indeed. Lasers are therefore employed in guiding missiles and aiming guns as well as in surveying.

Lasers are also used in compact disc players and videodisc systems to play back sound and pictures from the discs without touching them. The beam is reflected from the moving disc, which has the sound or pictures recorded on the surface in the form of a code. The laser beam takes up the code, which is then decoded to give the sound and pictures.

Lasers are also used to produce holograms.

RUBY LASER

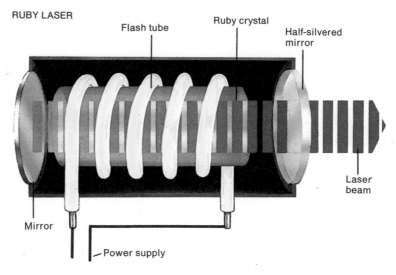

Flash tube • Ruby crystal • Half-silvered mirror • Laser beam • Mirror • Power supply

18% chromium

1% carbon

8% nickel

73% iron

STAINLESS STEEL

QUARTZ CRYSTALS

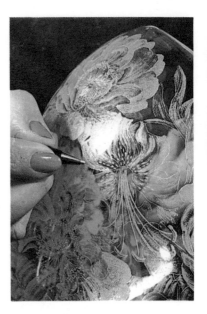

## ▲ WHAT IS THE DIFFERENCE BETWEEN A METAL AND AN ALLOY?

**A metal is a hard shiny substance like steel, copper or silver. Most metals are strong. Some metals, like copper and silver, are made of pure elements.**

**Alloys are metals that are mixtures of elements. Steel is an alloy of iron and carbon, often with other metals.**

In some cases, pure metals are useful. Most electric wire is made of pure copper or aluminium, for example.

But most of the metals that we use are alloys. This is because alloys can be made for particular uses in which pure metals are not very good. Pure iron is not very strong, so it is made into steel to give it strength. Other metals can then be added to steel to give it other qualities. Adding chromium and nickel produces stainless steel

Other alloys include brass, which is mainly made of copper and zinc, and bronze, made of copper and tin.

## ▲ WHAT ARE CRYSTALS?

**Crystals are substances like salt and sugar. Crystals form in certain shapes. Salt crystals are small cubes, for example. Many minerals like quartz form in crystals underground. Some are used as gems.**

Crystals form in certain shapes because their atoms or molecules are lined up in the same pattern of rows throughout the whole crystal.

A crystal can form when a liquid substance cools and solidifies, or when a solution of the substance evaporates so that the substance comes out of the solution. Salt crystals form as pools of sea water dry up, for example.

As the crystal forms, its atoms or molecules begin to line up in rows. As more atoms or molecules join them, the pattern gets larger and larger. This causes the crystal to grow in a particular shape.

Some crystals are used as gems. Jewellers cut and polish them to improve their appearance.

## ▲ WHAT IS THE HARDEST NATURAL SUBSTANCE ON EARTH?

**Diamond is the hardest natural substance on Earth. It is used in industry, for example in drilling and engraving. The glass shown here is being engraved with a diamond-tipped tool.**

Diamond is in fact an element. It is a very pure crystal form of carbon. Artificial diamonds are made from carbon by subjecting it to great heat and pressure. Real diamonds are formed underground in similar conditions.

Diamond is so strong because, when it forms, all the atoms throughout the crystal are linked together by very strong bonds.

To cut a diamond, it is necessary to cut through the bonds linking the carbon atoms together. This can be done by scratching the diamond with another diamond and then striking it to break it, or by using a diamond-tipped saw.

## ▼ WHAT IS SOUND?

**Sound is a form of energy. We detect it with our ears, just as we detect light energy with our eyes. Sound moves through air, water and many other substances. In air, it travels one kilometre in three seconds.**

Sound moves in waves. The waves consist of bands of high and low pressure, one after the other. As these bands of pressure strike your eardrums, they make them vibrate to and fro. This movement causes signals to go along nerves from your ears to your brain, and you hear the sound.

Sound waves are produced when objects vibrate quickly. This may be a vibrating string, as in a guitar or a violin, or a vibrating surface, as in a drum. When we talk or sing, the vocal cords in our throat vibrate to make sounds. The vibration sets up the bands of high and low pressure in the air, and the sound waves travel out in all directions.

Sound from climber — Sound returns to climber

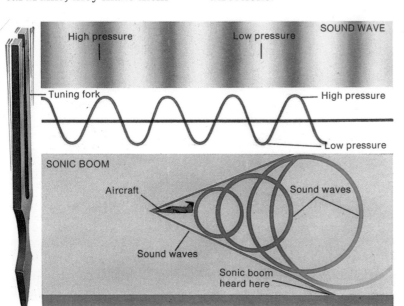

High pressure    Low pressure    SOUND WAVE

Tuning fork    High pressure
Low pressure

SONIC BOOM

Aircraft    Sound waves

Sound waves

Sonic boom heard here

## ▲ CAN AN AIRCRAFT FLY FASTER THAN THE SPEED OF SOUND?

**A supersonic aircraft can fly faster than the speed of sound. Aircraft do not usually fly faster than sound over land. This is because they produce a loud bang called a sonic boom as they pass overhead.**

The speed of sound is about 1200 kilometres per hour at sea level, but less high in the air.

The speed of sound at any height is known as Mach 1. Twice the speed of sound is Mach 2, and so on. When an aircraft is flying at the speed of sound or faster, it arrives at any point in the air before its own sound can get there.

The sound that it has been making suddenly arrives at once. The bands of pressure in the sound waves all travel together to give a very strong wave of air pressure called a shock wave. This wave travels out from the aircraft, producing a bang wherever it is heard.

## ▲ WHAT CAUSES AN ECHO?

**When you hear an echo of a sound, you hear the sound twice or more. What happens is that the sound waves bounce off a nearby wall or some other large surface. They reach your ears after the sound waves that have gone directly to your ears, and you hear an echo.**

When any sound is made, the sound waves travel out in all directions from the sound. You hear the sound as soon as the waves reach your ears.

But the waves also bounce off any surfaces that they reach, such as walls and ceilings. The sound waves come back to your ears and you hear the sound again.

In most places, the walls and ceiling are so near that the sound waves come back to you too quickly for you to hear the sound again. But if the walls or ceiling are some distance away, as in a cathedral or outside near large buildings or a cliff, the sound waves take a short time to return and you will hear an echo.

# OUT IN SPACE

▼ WHICH IS THE SMALLEST PLANET?

**Pluto is the smallest planet in the Solar System, but it is too far away for its diameter to be measured accurately. It is probably about 3000 kilometres across and is slightly smaller than the Moon. Pluto and its moon, Charon, are shown here to the right of Jupiter.**

Pluto's size is something of a mystery. It was discovered because of its gravitational pull on the other outer planets, Uranus and Neptune.

Astronomers expected Pluto's mass to be at least as great as the Earth's, whereas its true mass is about 1/60th of the Earth's. Is there another, much larger, planet awaiting discovery? Some astronomers believe that there is, but the search for it will be long and difficult.

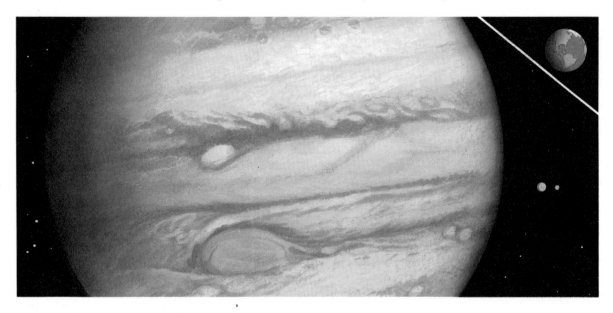

▲ WHICH IS THE LARGEST PLANET?

**Jupiter is the largest planet in the Solar System. It measures 142,800 kilometres across. It is so big that over a thousand Earths could be squashed inside it. Jupiter also contains about three times as much material as all the other planets put together!**

Although Jupiter is very large, it is not very dense. On the Earth's surface, an average cubic centimetre of Jupiter would weigh only 1.3 grams (not much more than water). An average cubic centimetre of our own planet would weigh 5.5 grams.

Jupiter is mostly pure hydrogen, although the surface we see contains compounds of hydrogen with other common elements such as nitrogen and carbon.

Jupiter's huge mass makes its gravitational pull very strong. Its outer satellites are over 20 million kilometres from its surface – 60 times the distance of our Moon. A body at this distance from the Earth would wander off into space. It would be attracted by the Sun and the other planets.

The core of Jupiter is very hot because of the pressure of its outer layers. If it had been about 20 times as massive, the centre would have grown hot enough for nuclear reactions to start. It would then have turned into a shining star instead of a frozen planet.

## ▼ WHICH PLANET IS THE HOTTEST?

**Strangely enough, it is not the closest to the Sun (Mercury) but the next closest: Venus. The surface temperature on Venus can rise to 480°C, which is much hotter than a baker's oven, and would be fatal to all known forms of life.**

Venus is hot because its thick atmosphere holds in the heat. But why are Venus and the Earth so different, when they are almost twins in size?

The atmosphere on Venus is mainly carbon dioxide, a choking gas and a very good heat blanket. The Earth may once have had a similar atmosphere but primitive life-forms broke it down into oxygen and carbon, letting the Sun's warmth escape.

This did not happen on Venus. Life did not develop, the blanket remained, and more and more carbon dioxide was roasted out of the surface rocks, making the temperature rise still higher. Venus became a baking inferno.

## ▲ WHICH PLANETS HAVE SATELLITES?

**Mercury and Venus are the only planets believed to be moonless. The Earth and Pluto have one satellite each. Mars and Neptune have two, Uranus has five, Jupiter has at least 14, and Saturn has over 20.**

Most satellites are too small to have an atmosphere, although Titan, in Saturn's family, is cloaked in nitrogen gas. Jupiter's Io has active volcanoes on its surface.

The largest satellite, Ganymede (5276 kilometres across), belongs to Jupiter. The smallest known satellite, Deimos (about 13 kilometres across), orbits around Mars.

Charon, with a diameter of about 1300 kilometres, is almost half the diameter of its parent planet Pluto. The smallest known satellites in Jupiter's family are about 20 kilometres across.

The illustration above shows Neptune and its moons Triton and Nereid. Triton is the larger of the two.

## ▲ WHICH PLANETS HAVE RINGS?

**Saturn's ring system has been known for centuries. Until recently, astronomers thought it was unique. In 1977, however, a faint ring system was discovered around Uranus, and in 1979 dim rings were found around Jupiter. It is possible that Neptune also has a ring.**

Saturn's rings are so large that they reflect more sunlight than the planet does. In a powerful telescope they look smooth, although the *Voyager* photographs show thousands of thin strands crowded together. Each strand contains countless icy particles.

Uranus, shown here, has at least nine separate ringlets. They are too faint to be seen from the Earth, but they can make a star flicker if they pass in front of it.

Jupiter has three ice-particle rings, and a fourth of sulphur vapour.

▼ WHAT IS A METEOR?

**A meteor, or shooting star, is a streak of light caused when an object no bigger than a pebble hurtles into the Earth's atmosphere from space and burns up. On most clear, moonless nights a meteor is seen every few minutes, but sometimes a hundred or more are seen every hour.**

These particles, known as meteoroids, have been orbiting the Sun for millions of years like separate tiny planets. They are invisible because they are so small. Some may be fragments left over after the planets were formed. Others may have been thrown out by comets; these usually travel in swarms, causing a meteor 'shower'.

To reach the ground as a meteorite, a meteoroid must have a mass of several kilograms. This is because a lot of material is burned off during its dive through the atmosphere at a speed of up to 50 kilometres a second.

▼ WHAT WAS THE LARGEST METEORITE TO FALL ON EARTH?

**A meteorite is the solid remains of a meteoroid that was large enough to survive its drop through the atmosphere. The largest known meteorite lies where it fell in Hoba West, Namibia, southwest Africa. It is over two metres across and weighs as much as 60 medium-size cars.**

We can be sure that much larger bodies have struck the Earth. About 90 ring-shaped features in different parts of the world could have been caused by huge impacts back in prehistoric times. For example, a three-kilometre diameter crater in Brazil was probably caused by an impact about 220 million years ago.

The best-known example of a meteorite crater is in Arizona. This 1.25-kilometre crater (shown here) was probably formed when a meteorite the size of a department store hit the Earth 25,000 years ago.

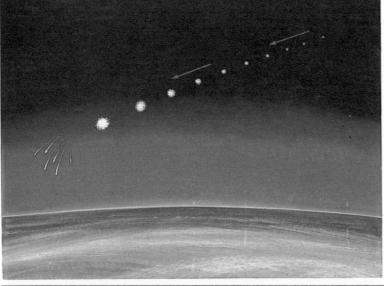

## ▶ WHAT IS AN ASTEROID?

**An asteroid, or 'minor planet', is a small body orbiting the Sun. The largest asteroid, Ceres (shown here compared in size to Italy), is only 1000 kilometres across. Others are much smaller.**

Over 2700 asteroids are now known. There is a zone between the orbits of Mars and Jupiter where most are found. But some can pass inside the Earth's orbit, and others go beyond Saturn.

## ◀ WHAT IS A COMET?

**A comet is an icy body just a few kilometres across, orbiting the Sun. Particles the size of dust and sand are mixed with the ice. When the comet passes near the Sun, the heat turns the ice to gas and the dust pours out into space, making the comet look hazy and perhaps giving it a long tail as well.**

Most known comets move in very elongated orbits, perhaps carrying them from the chilly zone beyond Jupiter to the hot regions of Venus and Mercury.

Comets are brightest when closest to the Sun, at *perihelion*. When farthest from the Sun, at *aphelion*, most comets are too faint to be seen from the Earth at all.

A comet grows enormously as it approaches perihelion, and tails are often millions of kilometres long. However, the dust is scattered so thinly that individual dust particles may be several kilometres apart.

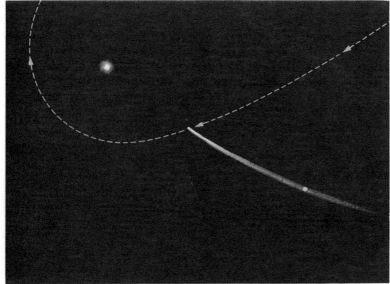

## ▲ WHAT WOULD HAPPEN IF A COMET HIT THE EARTH?

**Although a bright comet looks huge and impressive, the solid part is no bigger than a minor planet. So the chances of a serious collision are tiny, perhaps once in a hundred-million years.**

Even if a comet's nucleus did hit the Earth, it would not do as much harm as a collision with an asteroid of similar size. Comets seem to contain a lot of frozen liquid and dusty rock. But many asteroids contain solid rock and metal, so the impact would be more violent.

However, a comet's nucleus would blast a crater perhaps a hundred kilometres across, and spread destruction over a far wider area.

The Earth has passed through a comet's tail on many occasions. In 1910 the tail of Halley's Comet swept across our planet (as shown in the diagram), but it was so thin that no damage was caused.

### ▼ WHAT IS THE DIFFERENCE BETWEEN A STAR AND A PLANET?

**A star shines because its surface is very hot. But a planet has a cool surface and does not give out any light. The planets in the Solar System shine in the sky by reflecting sunlight. If the Sun stopped shining, the planets would be dark.**

Although astronomers have studied millions of stars, the only known planets are the ones circling the Sun.

It seems certain that many other stars have planetary systems, but even a very large planet orbiting a nearby star would be very faint indeed. It is possible that a star known as Barnard's Star has a planet, much more massive than Jupiter, orbiting around it. An invisible body seems to be exerting a gravitational pull on it, making it shift from side to side in the sky.

If both the Sun and nearby Barnard's Star have planets, the Galaxy must contain millions of solar systems. The picture shows a star with planets reflecting its light.

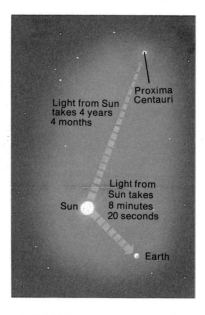

### ▲ HOW FAR AWAY IS THE NEAREST STAR?

**The nearest star to us is, of course, the Sun. Its average distance from the Earth is 149,600,000 kilometres. A beam of light, which travels through space at 300,000 kilometres per second, takes 8 minutes 20 seconds to reach us from the Sun. Light takes 4 years 4 months to travel from the Sun to its nearest neighbour star!**

It is easy to remember that this neighbour star, known as Proxima Centauri, is a quarter of a million times farther away than the Sun. If the Sun is represented by an orange 8 centimetres across, the Earth would be a speck less than a millimetre across and 8.5 metres away, while Proxima Centauri would be a slightly smaller orange over 2000 kilometres away.

Most of the stars that we see in the night sky are really brighter than the Sun. They appear faint to us only because they are so far away.

### ▼ WHICH IS THE LARGEST STAR?

**Even the largest stars look like tiny points of light when viewed with the largest telescopes, since they are so far away. Therefore it is very difficult to measure their diameters. One of the largest is Betelgeuse, the bright reddish star in Orion. Betelgeuse is shown here compared in size to the orbits of the inner planets.**

Betelgeuse is a red supergiant star. This class includes other prominent reddish stars, such as Antares in Scorpius and the bright star in Hercules known as Alpha Herculis. They are 15 to 20 times as massive as the Sun, but have puffed out to an enormous size. An average sample of a red supergiant would be less than a thousandth as dense as air.

Betelgeuse is surrounded by a shell of dust, probably thrown out from the star about 4500 years ago, and flying off into space at a speed of 10 kilometres per second.

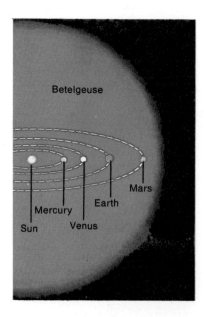

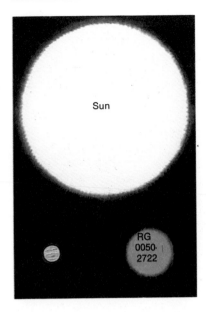

## ▲ WHICH IS THE SMALLEST STAR?

Ordinary small stars are very dim and hard to find. The smallest found so far is known as RG 0050–2722. It is about a quarter of the Sun's diameter, and 2.5 times the diameter of Jupiter, shown on its left. If it were placed at the centre of the Solar System, it would shine about as brightly as the Full Moon.

Many stars are known to be much smaller than RG 0050–2722, but these are not ordinary. They were once much larger than the Sun, but have grown old and collapsed into tiny bodies. Some are white dwarfs, which are the size of a planet such as Mars and much hotter than the Sun. Others are the neutron stars, which are only a few kilometres across and so dense that a pin's head of their material would weigh about a million tonnes.

Very small, dim stars will never reach this state, but will glow quietly on for thousands of millions of years.

## ▼ WHAT IS A VARIABLE STAR?

**A variable star changes in brightness. Some take a few hours, while others may take many years. Most are swelling and shrinking, becoming brighter and fainter as they do so. Others are pairs of stars, which seem to change in brightness when one passes in front of the other.**

This second type of variable star is known as an eclipsing binary, and the light-changes are repeated very accurately.

Most of the truly variable stars are giants – very large stars that are more massive than the Sun. These often brighten and fade again in a cycle lasting about a year, and during this time their light output can change by thousands of times. They are known as long-period variables, or LPVs.

The Sun, fortunately, seems to have shone steadily for most of its lifetime of 4600 million years, like other stars of its type.

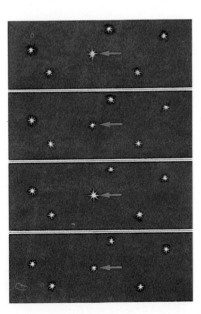

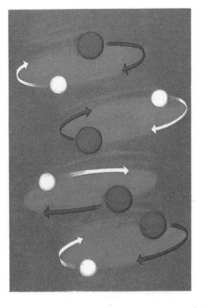

## ▲ WHAT IS A BINARY STAR?

**A binary star consists of two stars revolving around each other. The closer they are, the faster they will revolve. Some binaries take just a few hours to go round once, while others take thousands of years.**

About a quarter of all known stars belong to binary systems. Most of these, particularly the close pairs, must have been born as twins, since the chances of two stars passing near each other and being 'caught' are tiny indeed.

Some binary pairs consist of similar stars. In other cases one star is large, cool and reddish, and the other star is small and white-hot, perhaps even lying inside the 'atmosphere' of its companion.

If the Sun had a neighbour, similar to itself, at the distance of the Earth, the two stars would revolve around each other in about 8.5 months. At the distance of Mercury, the period would be about 8 weeks.

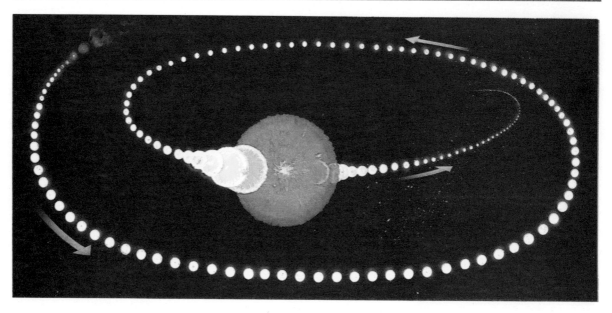

## ▲ WHAT ARE RED GIANTS AND WHITE DWARFS?

**When a star is born, it usually shines steadily for hundreds of millions of years. But eventually many stars begin to puff outwards as a fiery mist. This is the red giant stage. Finally, they shrink into a very hot globe the size of a planet – a white dwarf.**

If the Sun ever becomes a red giant, the inner planets will disappear beneath its surface and scorch. But this will not happen for thousands of millions of years, because the Sun is not a very massive star.

The more mass (material) a star has, the faster it develops, and the red giants that we see in the Galaxy are all more massive than the Sun. Since red giants are very luminous, they are easy to detect at a great distance.

But white dwarfs are dim, only one-hundredth the luminosity of the Sun. Astronomers have been able to discover only a few, although they must be very common indeed.

## ▼ WHAT IS A CONSTELLATION?

**Constellations in early times were simply patterns of stars in the sky. They were named after ancient gods, heroes and animals. Examples of constellations are Orion the Hunter (shown here) and Leo the Lion.**

There are now 88 constellations over the whole sky. Twelve of them form a wide track where the Sun appears to travel in the course of the year, and where the planets are usually found. These are the zodiacal constellations.

About 45 constellations, especially the ones that can be seen from most of the northern hemisphere, were first named thousands of years ago. But there is a large group of 'modern' constellations, particularly in the southern sky, which were not charted until the great sea voyages of the 17th and 18th centuries took place.

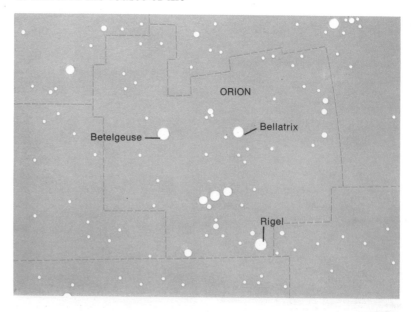

ORION

Betelgeuse

Bellatrix

Rigel

## ▼ WHAT ARE NOVAE AND SUPERNOVAE?

**Both of these objects are exploding stars, which erupt almost overnight. Several novae occur in our Galaxy every year, and some can be seen with the naked eye. A bright nova was seen in the constellation of Cygnus, the Swan, in 1975. A supernova is much more violent, and rare. The last one was seen in 1604.**

All novae seem to be close binary stars. The outburst, which can raise the brightness of the binary by 10,000 times, is caused by gas from one star pouring on to its companion.

A supernova (arrowed in the illustration) is a single star several times more massive than the Sun. It becomes so hot inside that the outer layers cannot hold in the tremendous radiation. For a few days, it sends out as much energy as a whole galaxy of thousands of millions of stars. A supernova in 1054 could be seen in daylight, but its remains, the Crab Nebula, are now only a dim blur.

## ▼ WHAT IS A PULSAR?

**After a supernova explosion, all that is left of a star is a very hot ball of matter a few kilometres across, spinning at a tremendous rate. It sends out a beam of light or radio waves like a revolving searchlight, so that it seems to 'pulse' on and off. It is called a pulsar.**

These remains are the shrunken core of the original star, at a temperature of millions of degrees.

One of the strongest pulsars is the star at the centre of the Crab Nebula, which rotates 30 times a second. The fastest known pulsar, however, rotates 642 times a second.

All pulsars are gradually slowing down as they lose energy, and one estimate is that after about four million years they will be spinning too slowly for the beaming effect to be noticeable.

Most pulsars are too faint to be seen except with a very large telescope, but they emit radio waves very powerfully. In fact, they were discovered by radio observations.

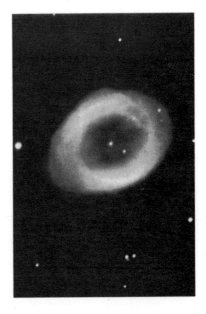

## ▲ WHAT IS A NEBULA?

**A nebula is an enormous cloud of gas atoms and tiny particles. Even the smallest nebulae are much larger than the Solar System, while the largest are hundreds of light-years across. New stars are formed inside nebulae. Some dying stars throw out nebulae.**

Some nebulae appear bright, while others are dark. The bright ones are either reflecting starlight, or glow because their atoms are affected by the energy given out by nearby stars. The Ring Nebula is shown here. Dark nebulae appear as black starless areas, since they are absorbing light from stars beyond.

Normal nebulae are so thin that the Earth could pass through one without our noticing anything unusual. But there are so many in our Galaxy, and they are so huge, that there is probably as much material in them as in the stars. Some contain small dark spots, which are new stars being formed.

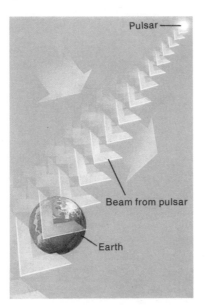

Pulsar

Beam from pulsar

Earth

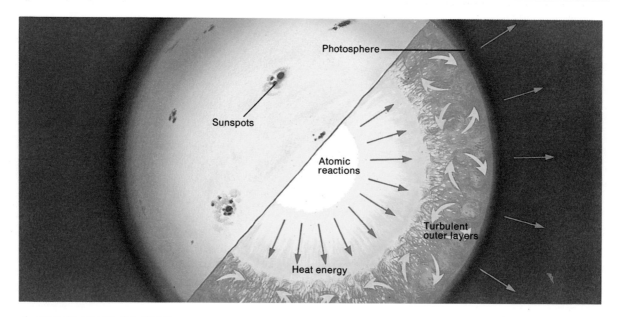

Photosphere

Sunspots

Atomic
reactions

Turbulent
outer layers

Heat energy

### ▲ WHAT SORT OF STAR IS THE SUN?

**The Sun belongs to a family of about 100,000 million stars in our Galaxy. Some are much hotter than the Sun, while others are cooler. Some are much larger, and some are smaller. The Sun is a very ordinary star, and there are millions of other stars like it.**

To us, the Sun is special because it controls a family of planets. Although we cannot hope to detect planets around other stars by trying to see them, there is good evidence that other stars may have planetary families.

This is because some stars rotate, like the Sun, very slowly, with a period of several weeks. A normal single star should be rotating in a few hours, but the pull of the planets has slowed it down. These other, slowly-rotating stars may also have planets revolving around them.

### ▲ WHAT IS A SUNSPOT?

**A sunspot is a dark area on the Sun's brilliant surface. It appears dark because it is cooler, and so gives out less light. Sunspots are particularly common every 11 years or so, and this is known as the sunspot cycle.**

Sunspots indicate regions of intense magnetic activity below the Sun's surface, or photosphere. This magnetic force pierces the surface and arches invisibly into space. The photosphere is heated by atomic reactions deep inside the Sun. But the magnetic field blocks some of this heat, causing the centre of a sunspot to be about 1500°C cooler than the rest of the surface.

Sunspots often occur in pairs, one at each base of the magnetic arch. Some groups have lasted for months, and can extend for ten times the Earth's diameter. These can be seen with the naked eye, but a proper filter *must* be used, not film or smoked glass.

### ▲ HOW HOT IS THE SUN?

**The Sun is hottest at its centre, where the temperature is believed to be about 15 million degrees Centigrade. By the time this heat has worked its way to the surface, it has fallen to 6000 degrees – about four times as hot as a steel furnace. Many stars are hotter than the Sun.**

The coolest known stars have a surface temperature of about 2000 degrees, while the hottest are about 50,000 degrees. The hotter an object is, the bluer is the light it emits. Very cool stars are reddish, and very hot ones are bluish-white. The Sun is yellowish.

Strangely enough, the thin hydrogen layer above the visible surface of the Sun, known as the chromosphere, has a temperature of about 10,000 degrees. This is because energy from beneath the surface is carried up in the form of sound waves, which fade out in the thin chromosphere and turn this energy into heat.

## ▼ WHAT CAUSES AURORAE?

**At about 200 kilometres above the Earth's surface, the air is very thin and its atoms are widely scattered. Tiny electric particles from space, known as electrons, can penetrate the air at this height. If one strikes an atom, a flash of light is given out. An aurora is the glow caused by countless millions of these flashes, produced when the Sun is very active.**

The electrons which produce aurorae do not come directly from the Sun, but from an invisible layer of electrons around the Earth known as the Van Allen belt.

Particles from the Sun cause these electrons to shoot down into the atmosphere. They follow the Earth's magnetic field, which usually guides them towards the North and South Poles, where most aurorae occur. There were many aurorae when the Sun was active in 1980 and 1981.

## ▲ WHAT IS THE SUN'S CORONA?

**The corona is often called the Sun's atmosphere, but it is not at all like our own atmosphere. It has a temperature of a million degrees Centigrade, and is a million times thinner than air. The brilliance of the Sun hides it from view except during a total eclipse, as seen here.**

The corona contains atoms of hydrogen, nitrogen, oxygen, iron and other common elements. They are so hot, and are scattered so far apart, that they have lost some of their electrons, which fly about.

During a total eclipse, the corona seems to extend for one or two Sun-diameters into space (about two million kilometres). In fact, it extends out beyond the region of the Earth as a rapid outflow of atomic particles called the solar wind. The shape of the corona changes with the sunspot cycle. It is fairly regular at minimum activity, and butterfly-shaped at maximum.

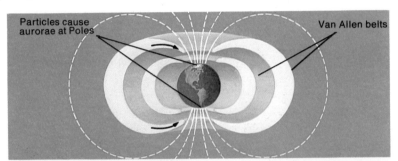

Particles cause aurorae at Poles

Van Allen belts

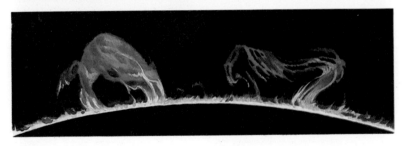

## ▲ WHAT ARE SOLAR PROMINENCES?

**A prominence is a fountain of glowing gas rising up from the Sun's surface. Some prominences escape into space, but most last for a few hours or days, and then fall back into the Sun.**

Prominences appear bright when seen during a total eclipse, poking up from the edge of the black disc of the Moon, as shown here. But they are dimmer than the photosphere, and cannot normally be seen without special equipment.

Most prominences are far larger than the Earth. In fact, a hundred Earths could be fitted beneath a large arched prominence. But the gas in them is very thin, only a thousandth as dense as air.

Some prominences are expelled from the photosphere at speeds of 200 kilometres a second, or even more. These 'eruptive' prominences may be formed differently from the 'quiescent' type.

79

### ▼ WHAT IS THE MILKY WAY?

**If the night is very clear and there is no Moon, a hazy band of light can be seen running through some of the constellations. This band is caused by distant stars, which cannot be seen separately with the naked eye.**

The Milky Way is the proof, to the naked eye, of the shape of the Galaxy in which the Sun is located. If the Galaxy were spherical in shape, we should see distant, faint stars in all directions in the sky.

The Milky Way effect suggests that the Galaxy must be flattened in form, like many other galaxies that can be observed with powerful telescopes.

The brightest part of the Milky Way lies in the constellation of Sagittarius, the Archer. Here, we are looking towards the centre of the Galaxy. There is another bright region in Perseus, where we are looking at a nearby spiral arm. Dark nebulae, which block out light, cause the patchiness.

### ▼ WHAT TYPES OF GALAXY ARE THERE?

**No two galaxies look exactly alike, but there are three main kinds. Some are irregular, with no particular shape (top). Others are spiral, like our own, with trailing arms of stars and nebulae (middle). The commonest are elliptical, like a smooth swarm of stars (bottom).**

Stars are formed out of gas and dust, and the amount of star-forming matter in a galaxy tells us something about its development.

Elliptical galaxies have little or no free gas and dust left, so that no new stars can be formed. They usually contain many old red giant stars.

Spiral and irregular galaxies have both old and young stars, and reserves of material to make new stars. In spiral systems the centre, or nucleus, consists of red giants, and star formation is going on only in the dusty arms. Elliptical galaxies may be former spirals which have lost their arms.

### ▼ WHICH IS THE NEAREST GALAXY TO OUR OWN?

**Our Galaxy's closest neighbour is the Large Magellanic Cloud (seen here) which is about 150,000 light-years away. It is only one-third the diameter of our Galaxy, and contains only a tenth as many stars. The Small Magellanic Cloud is about 190,000 light-years away.**

The nearest spiral galaxy like our own is the Andromeda galaxy, over two million light-

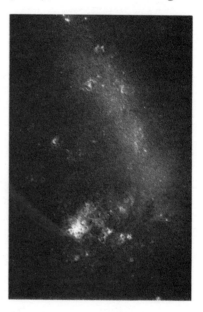

years away. Like the Magellanic Clouds, it can be seen with the naked eye.

All these galaxies belong to the Local Group, a cluster of about 24 galaxies. Ours and the Andromeda galaxy are the largest members. Most of the others are small, faint elliptical systems. The irregular Magellanic Clouds are satellites of our own Galaxy. The nearest independent galaxy is a tiny object only 3000 light-years across and 250,000 light-years away.

## ▼ WHAT IS A QUASAR?

**Quasars are very distant, very powerful objects. They seem to be much smaller than true galaxies, but send out much more energy. The most distant known quasars are much farther off than the most remote galaxies that have been observed. They are at least 10,000 million light-years away.**

Some unusual galaxies known as Seyferts have very bright centres, and quasars may be

galaxies with some fantastically powerful energy source at their centre.

Recent evidence has suggested that some quasars are surrounded by ordinary stars. Quasars send out very strong radio waves and X-rays but are so faint in visible light that, to us, they appear like faint stars. All quasars are thousands of millions of light-years away, and so we see them now as they were that length of time ago. There are no 'young' quasars.

## ▲ WHAT IS THE AGE OF THE UNIVERSE?

**The galaxies in the universe appear to be expanding away from each other. If we work backwards, we find that they were close together between 15,000 and 20,000 million years ago. Is this when the universe began?**

Most astronomers agree that the galaxies are flying away from some explosion that 'created' the universe. But it is impossible to say why this explosion, or 'Big Bang' occurred. But scientists have calculated what could have been happening less than a millionth of a second after the Bang!

Also, not all astronomers agree about the age of the universe. Recent work has suggested an age of about 10,000 million years, but this seems to be less than the ages of the oldest stars in the Galaxy.

It is also possible that the Bang marked a new explosion of a previous universe that had expanded and contracted.

## ▲ HOW WILL THE UNIVERSE END?

**Nobody knows – yet. The galaxies may go on flying apart for ever. However, they might begin to slow down, come to a halt, and then fly inwards to the 'Big Crunch'. At the moment, astronomers cannot make sufficiently accurate observations to decide.**

The future of the universe depends upon the amount of material it contains. The greater the amount of material, the more powerful is the gravitational force trying to pull the galaxies back together. It is similar to launching a spacecraft. The more massive the planet, the faster the spacecraft must move to escape into space.

The galaxies we observe do not seem massive enough to end the expansion of the universe. But they may contain hidden mass, in the form of dust or even atomic particles, which will eventually slow down and end the present expansion.

81

# PLANET EARTH

▼ WHAT IS A YEAR?

**A year is the time it takes the Earth to travel round the Sun. As the Earth travels, it rotates on its axis. We call one complete revolution a day. The Earth takes just over 365 days to orbit the Sun.**

One complete orbit of the Earth round the Sun is called the solar year. This lasts 365 days, 5 hours, 48 minutes, 46 seconds (nearly $365\frac{1}{4}$ days).

The calendar year is divided into 365 days, slightly less than the solar year. So an extra day is added every fourth year (the leap year) to make up for the difference.

Leap years occur in every year whose number can be divided by four, for example 1984, 1988, 1992. This rule does not apply to the first year of a century unless it can be divided by 400. So the year 2000 will be a leap year.

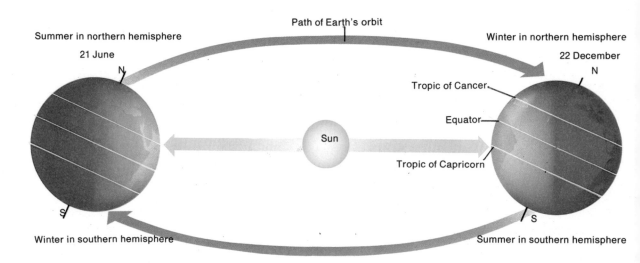

Summer in northern hemisphere
21 June
N

Path of Earth's orbit

Winter in northern hemisphere
22 December
N

Tropic of Cancer
Equator
Sun
Tropic of Capricorn

S

Winter in southern hemisphere

S

Summer in southern hemisphere

▲ WHAT ARE THE TROPICS?

**The Tropics are imaginary lines on the Earth's surface where the Sun is exactly overhead at mid-day in midsummer. At mid-day on 21 June the Sun is overhead at the Tropic of Cancer. At mid-day on 22 December the Sun is overhead at the Tropic of Capricorn.**

The Tropic of Cancer and the Tropic of Capricorn are lines of latitude parallel to the Equator. The latitude of a place is measured by the angle formed between the place, the centre of the Earth and the Equator. The Tropics are latitudes $23\frac{1}{2}°$ north and south of the Equator.

The Earth's axis is not vertical in relation to the path it takes round the Sun. It is tilted at $23\frac{1}{2}°$ off vertical.

As the diagram shows, in June the North Pole is pointing towards the Sun. On midsummer's day in the northern hemisphere, the Sun is exactly overhead at mid-day at latitude $23\frac{1}{2}°$ north – the Tropic of Cancer. In December it is the South Pole which points towards the Sun. On midsummer's day in the southern hemisphere, the Sun is exactly overhead at mid-day at latitude $23\frac{1}{2}°$ south – the Tropic of Capricorn.

Land and sea between the two Tropics are called tropical. Here, the Sun is overhead twice in the year. The Sun's heat is most concentrated in this part of the world, and the climate is hot all year.

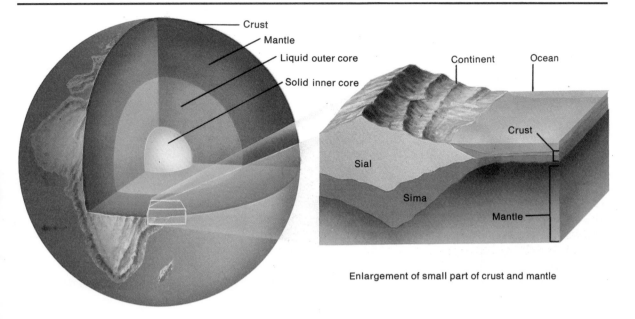

Enlargement of small part of crust and mantle

### ▲ WHAT SHAPE IS THE EARTH?

**Our planet is not a perfect sphere. It is slightly flattened at the poles, and even the Equator is not an exact circle.**

New information from satellites has agreed with measurements made on the surface of the Earth. So scientists now have more details of the Earth's shape.

The Earth's circumference at the Equator is 40,075.03 kilometres and its circumference through the Poles is 40,007.89 kilometres. Its diameter at the Equator is 12,756.28 kilometres and its diameter at the Poles is 12,713.51 kilometres.

The variations are because of flattening at the Poles and bulging at the Equator. This is partly the result of the fact that the Earth spins so fast. The Equator itself is slightly oval: its longest diameter is 159 metres longer than its shortest diameter! The South Pole is 45 metres nearer the centre of the Earth than the North Pole.

### ▲ WHAT IS THE EARTH MADE OF?

**From studying earthquakes and the Earth's gravity, scientists know that the Earth is made of a number of layers.**

The Earth's crust is the thinnest zone of all. It varies in thickness from five kilometres under parts of the oceans to 40 kilometres under the continents. The rocks of the continents are lighter than the rocks of the ocean floors, but all are rich in silicon.

The top layer of the mantle may be rigid, but the rest consists of molten rocks which are slowly moving. The rocks of the different layers of the mantle are rich in magnesium and iron silicates.

About 2900 kilometres beneath the Earth's surface is the divide between the mantle and the core. The outer core is probably liquid, while the inner core is solid. The rocks of the core are probably 90 per cent iron with some nickel, similar to many meteorites.

### ▲ WHAT IS THE CRUST LIKE BENEATH THE CONTINENTS AND OCEANS?

**The rocks of the continents vary but on average they are much less dense than the rocks of the ocean floor. The rocks under the oceans also continue deep beneath the rocks of the continents.**

The rocks of the continents are mostly granite, or are made from sediments which come from granite. They are rich in silicon and aluminium. All the rocks of the continents are grouped together as *sial*.

The rocks beneath the deep oceans are very like basalt. They are rich in silicon and magnesium, and are grouped together as *sima*.

The Earth's crust consists of a layer of sima above the mantle. The continents are huge 'rafts' of sial floating in the sima. So it is possible for the continents to move apart or together (continental drift) and to move up and down (isostacy).

83

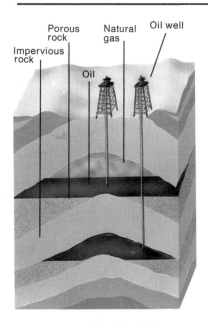

Impervious rock
Porous rock
Natural gas
Oil well
Oil

## ▼ WHAT IS A FOSSIL?

**A fossil is the remains of an animal or a plant preserved in the rocks.**

There are many ways in which plants and animals that lived hundreds of millions of years ago have been preserved. A few fossils are the hard parts of animals or plants, such as dinosaur bones or sharks' teeth. These remains sank to the bottom of seas and were trapped in the sediments, which now form layers of rock.

Many fossils are moulds or casts. The remains of living things slowly dissolved as they lay buried in sediments. Their exact shape was preserved in the rocks that formed. Minerals or sediments took the place of their remains to form a cast. Some ancient trees were 'petrified' as the decaying logs were gradually replaced by minerals dissolved in water.

Interesting details can be fossilized, too. Footprints, once made on mud which then dried out, may be uncovered.

## ▲ WHAT ARE OIL AND NATURAL GAS?

**Oil and natural gas are fossil fuels. They formed from the remains of tiny plants and animals which once lived in tropical seas. They were changed by chemical processes into gases and liquids.**

Oil and natural gas formed from different kinds of micro-scopic plant and animal remains, at different depths in the Earth, at different temperatures, and over different periods of time.

Oil varies in type from a very light oil to thick, black bitumen. Natural gas also varies in type and quality. Different types of oil may be mixed at refineries, which produce paraffin, petroleum, diesel oil and chemicals.

As the diagram shows, oil and gas collect in porous rocks (rocks which allow liquids to soak through). They are trapped between impervious rocks (which will not allow liquids to pass through). Some oil wells pump oil from a huge area. Others tap only a small area and soon run dry.

Fossil leaf imprint on coal

## ▲ WHAT IS COAL?

**Coal is a rock which can be burned as a fuel. It is called a 'fossil fuel' because it formed from the remains of trees and plants millions of years ago. Imprints of these plants can be found on some lumps of coal.**

Coal is usually found in layers (called seams) of different thicknesses sandwiched between other rocks which formed at the same time. This suggests that dead vegetation collected in swamps. This was buried by mud and silt. Then new swamp forests grew and eventually they too were buried. These layers of vegetation, mud and silt eventually became coal seams between sandstone and clay.

The oldest known coal seams are about 360 million years old. Then coal is found in rocks of all different ages until less than 70 million years ago. The most valuable coal in Europe and North America is found in Carboniferous rocks formed 265 to 290 million years ago.

## ▼ WHAT IS A MINERAL?

**A mineral is a single substance that is formed naturally. Different samples of the same mineral usually look similar and react in the same way when they are tested. Rocks are made up of different minerals.**

There are over 3000 different minerals known today. Each one has its own chemical formula. Mineralogists group minerals into 'families' such as micas, feldspars, quartz and calcites.

All minerals (except mercury) are solids, though they melt under enormous heat and pressure. As they cool down again, most minerals can form crystals. Some minerals make up the common rocks of the Earth's surface. Some rare minerals are valuable (such as gold and diamonds).

Collectors identify minerals by their crystal shape, their hardness, the way they break, and the colour of the mark they make when scratching a white surface.

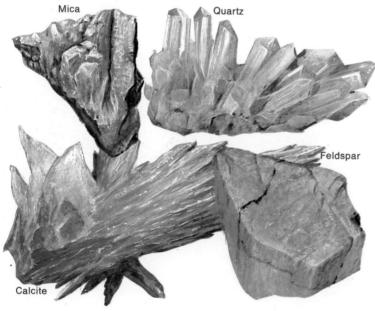

Mica

Quartz

Feldspar

Calcite

## ▲ WHAT ARE THE MOST COMMON ROCK-FORMING MINERALS?

**The majority of minerals found in the rocks of the Earth's crust are silicates.**

The Earth's crust is made up of different kinds of rocks. Igneous rocks formed as molten lava cooled down. Most sedimentary rocks formed from accumulations of minerals which were weathered out of igneous rocks. Sometimes the minerals in these rocks can be seen quite easily, for example in granite and in gritstone. Sometimes the minerals can only be seen under a microscope. In either case, most of the minerals you will see are silicates.

The silicates are a large group of minerals, all of which contain silica and oxygen. The commonest silicate families are feldspars (about 60 per cent of rock-forming minerals), amphiboles and pyroxenes (about 17 per cent), quartz (about 12 per cent) and micas (about 4 per cent).

## ▼ WHICH ROCKS ARE USED FOR BUILDING?

**Rocks are used as building materials because they resist weathering. Usually such rocks are hard and often they are beautiful too. Rocks that are easily quarried and shaped for building are especially important. Softer rocks such as clay and sand are dug up and made into harder building materials such as bricks and concrete.**

Many old buildings are built of local stone or bricks. When transport was difficult, only the richest people could afford to import special stone.

Now that stone can be transported easily, modern buildings may be made with rocks from far away. Building materials made from clay, limestone, sand and gravel are the most common.

Impressive buildings are often built or faced with hard-wearing rocks such as metamorphic rocks. These have been naturally hardened by heat and pressure. They include marble and slate.

## ▼ WHAT EFFECTS CAN EARTHQUAKES HAVE?

**Earthquakes strike without warning. They are heard first as a great rumble. Strong earthquakes cause enormous damage in built-up areas.**

Buildings collapse, and fractured pipes and cables cause fires. Rescue services are hampered by lack of communications. Landslides may increase the damage, and cause flooding. *Tsunami*, or tidal waves, may devastate the coast, and also do great damage thousands of kilometres away.

Earthquakes are most violent at a point on the Earth's surface immediately above the place where the Earth's crust has moved.

The most destructive earthquakes are 'shallow focus'. These are earthquakes that begin less than 60 kilometres beneath the surface. Sometimes the land at the surface is cracked and displaced after an earthquake.

Several thousand earthquakes are recorded by seismographs every year.

## ▼ WHAT DIFFERENT KINDS OF VOLCANO ARE THERE?

**Volcanoes can be classed as active, dormant (sleeping) or extinct. Active volcanoes vary in shape.**

Fluid lava usually wells up fairly slowly, giving plenty of time for any gases to escape. Such volcanic eruptions are peaceful, but the fluid lava may flow long distances to form a very large volcano with a gently sloping dome.

Thicker lava traps gas

bubbles which may burst at the surface and send up a shower of lava and volcanic 'bombs'. These explosive eruptions make a lot of ash and form steep-sided cinder cones which often have a beautifully symmetrical shape.

Really thick lava hardly flows at all. It is squeezed out of the volcano like toothpaste from a tube. Sometimes such lava forms a volcanic plug. Gases build up inside, and may eventually make the whole volcano explode.

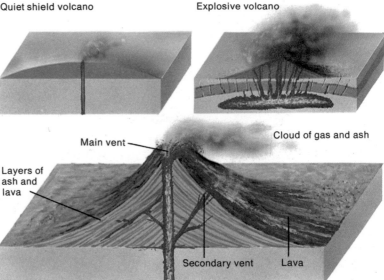

Quiet shield volcano

Explosive volcano

Cloud of gas and ash

Main vent

Layers of ash and lava

Secondary vent    Lava

## ▲ WHAT EFFECTS CAN VOLCANIC ERUPTIONS HAVE?

**Eruptions vary according to the type of magma produced. Besides the burning lava, ash and gas may affect large areas. An eruption may cause earthquakes and landslides. A violent eruption may destroy land, or may bring a new island to the surface.**

The recent eruptions of Mount St Helens in the north-west USA have been

recorded in great detail by scientists. When eruptions began in 1980, an earthquake triggered off a landslide. Immediately, a blast of hot gases and steam flattened forests up to 27 kilometres away. Blast after blast sent ash and rocks high into the air.

Valleys were buried, and people and animals choked to death. Floods and mudflows did more damage. A great ash storm, with lightning, turned daylight to night 140 kilometres away. Towns were choked with ash, and beautiful sunsets followed.

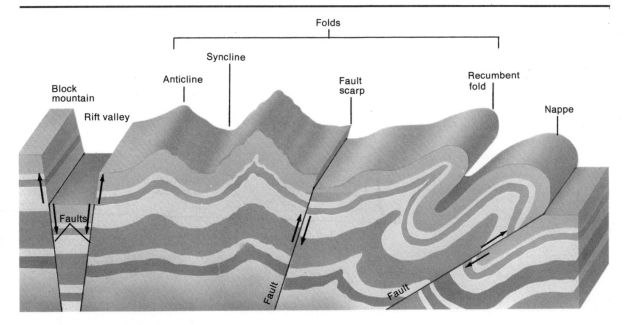

Folds — Syncline — Anticline — Fault scarp — Recumbent fold — Nappe — Block mountain — Rift valley — Faults — Fault — Fault

## ▲ WHAT DIFFERENT KINDS OF MOUNTAIN ARE THERE?

**The three main types of mountain are volcanoes, fold mountains and block (or faulted ) mountains.**

Volcanoes are the only mountains formed from new material added to the Earth's surface.

Fold mountains are formed when great areas of sedimentary rocks are pushed together. The rocks are folded, crushed and pushed up to make mountain ranges such as the Alps and the Jura. Such ranges probably formed when continents moved against one another, or against part of the ocean floor.

Block mountains are formed when great areas of rocks are faulted, and some areas are pushed up between the faults. Rift valleys (formed when an area slips down between faults) often occur with block mountains. For example, the Vosges and the Black Forest are block mountains on either side of the Rhine rift valley.

## ▲ WHAT DO GEOLOGISTS MEAN BY 'FOLDING'?

**Most rocks may seem very hard. But when pressure is applied from one or both sides, layers of rock can be bent into folds.**

If you push this page gently towards the centre of the book it will arch up into an 'upfold'. Moderate pressure produces gentle folds in rocks. Upfolds are called anticlines and downfolds are called synclines. Uneven pressure produces folds with one side steeper than the other. These are called asymmetrical folds.

Intense pressure can crumple the rocks, producing dramatic folds and faults so that one part of a fold may be pushed over another.

Folds can sometimes be seen on mountainsides or cliff-faces. They vary greatly in size and are formed very slowly.

The pressure needed to create folds probably comes from the movement of parts of the Earth's crust against each other.

## ▲ WHAT DO GEOLOGISTS MEAN BY 'FAULTS'?

**Faults are great cracks through layers of rocks. Pressure on the cracks causes movement, which is felt as an earthquake. This usually results in the rock layers being displaced on each side of the fault.**

Faults cross strata (layers) of different kinds of rock. They are caused by enormous pressure pushing or pulling the rock strata, which break under the great stress. Faults are often found with folds.

Areas of rock may shift up or down on each side of the fault. This may cause a fault scarp in the landscape, but often faults are hardly visible.

Movement along a fault can be quite small-scale and you may see faults in road-cuttings or cliffs. There can also be large-scale movements, such as along the faults on either side of the Great Rift Valley. This stretches for 4800 kilometres through parts of the Middle East and eastern Africa.

87

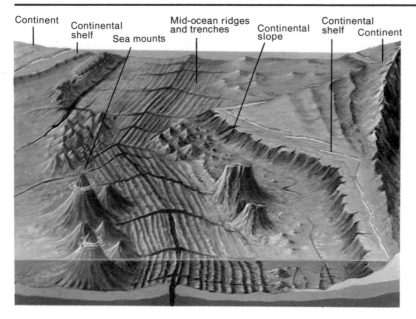

Continent · Continental shelf · Sea mounts · Mid-ocean ridges and trenches · Continental slope · Continental shelf · Continent

## ▲ WHAT IS THE CONTINENTAL SHELF?

**The continental shelf is the true edge of the continents. All round the continents, the sea floor slopes gently away from present-day beaches. Where the depth of the sea is about 180 metres, this gentle slope ends abruptly at the steep continental slope.**

The width of the continental shelf varies enormously, for example, around South America. There is hardly any continental shelf off the coast of Chile. The steep slope of the Andes is matched by a steep drop into the ocean depths. But off Argentina the continental shelf stretches far into the Atlantic, east of the Falkland Islands.

The continental shelf is valuable. The shallow waters are often rich in fish. Sands and gravels accumulating as sediments on the sea floor are dredged up in some places. Sometimes they include minerals such as gold and diamonds.

## ◄ WHAT DOES THE SEA BED LOOK LIKE?

**The sea bed has cliffs, plateaus, canyons, volcanoes, mountain ranges and deep trenches.**

Echo-sounders, underwater cameras, manned and unmanned submersibles are helping oceanographers know more about the sea bed.

There are three main zones. The continental shelf slopes gently away from the beaches surrounding dry land. At a depth of about 180 metres, it suddenly ends at the steep continental slope. This huge cliff around the continents is gashed with deep gorges and sediments pile up at its foot.

The deep ocean floor begins at the bottom of the continental slope. Submerged volcanoes rise up in places. Some reach the surface, as at Hawaii and the Canary Islands. Mountain ranges such as the Mid-Atlantic Ridge are far longer than any mountain ranges on land. There are also deep, narrow trenches such as Challenger Deep, the lowest place on Earth.

---

Spring tide · Full Moon · Earth · New Moon · Sun

Neap tide · Quarter Moon · Earth · Quarter Moon · Sun

Arrows show pull of gravity on oceans

## ◄ WHAT ARE SPRING AND NEAP TIDES?

**Spring tides have the greatest tidal range, with the highest high tides and the lowest low tides. Neap tides have the least tidal range. Tides are partly caused by the Moon, and are related to its phases. Each type of tide occurs twice in every lunar month (28 days).**

The water of the oceans is kept on the Earth's surface by the pull of the Earth's gravity.

But it does respond to the pull of gravity of the Moon and the Sun. The Moon orbits the Earth in one lunar month. Near Full Moon and New Moon, the pull of gravity of the Sun and Moon are in the same direction (top diagram), causing particularly high and low spring tides.

When the pull of the Sun and the Moon are in different directions (lower diagram), neap tides occur. They coincide with the Moon's first and last quarters.

### ▶ WHAT IS A 'TSUNAMI'?

*Tsunami* **is a Japanese word meaning 'over-flowing' (*tsu*) 'wave' (*nami*). A *tsunami* is caused by earthquake shocks.**

Shock-waves from an earthquake affect the sea floor as well as the land. A major earthquake can make the sea floor rise and fall and create huge sea waves. If these reach coasts, they swamp large areas and cause great damage.

At sea, *tsunamis* have long wavelengths. The distance from one wave crest to the next may be 200 kilometres. They travel quickly, at up to 800 kilometres an hour. Where the sea bed gets shallower, they slow down but become higher. From the land, people may see the sea withdraw a long way, then rush up in a series of giant waves.

In the 1755 earthquake at Lisbon, Portugal, the harbour was emptied of water. Then waves 17 metres high added to the devastation already caused by the earthquake.

### ▶ WHAT ARE ICEBERGS?

**Icebergs are huge lumps of ice which have broken away from ice sheets and glaciers and drift in the sea. When ice floats in water, only about a ninth shows above the surface. The rest is hidden beneath the water, and may damage ships.**

In the northern hemisphere, icebergs come from the Greenland ice sheet. The world's tallest iceberg, 167 metres high, was sighted off western Greenland in 1958.

The largest icebergs are found in the southern hemisphere and come from Antarctica. The largest ever recorded was 335 kilometres long and 97 kilometres wide (31,000 square kilometres in area). It was measured in the South Pacific in 1956.

Icebergs may break from a glacier and fall into the sea. Usually, icebergs form from a glacier which extends into the sea. Waves, tides and floating movement of the ice cause huge pieces of ice to break off and float away.

Tip of iceberg above ocean

### ▶ WHAT IS A RAISED BEACH?

**The photograph seems to show a beach with boats drawn up on the sand. But there is rock instead of sea! In fact, this beach is raised above high-tide mark. Either the land has risen or the sea-level has dropped.**

A change of sea-level sounds the simplest answer, but the world's ice is still slowly melting, so sea-level ought to be getting higher, not lower.

But ice is a key to the answer. Sea-level has changed a great deal in the past million years as the amount of ice has increased and decreased. Some high-level beaches were formed when the climate was warmer. Sea-level was higher than it is now because there was little ice in the world.

Other raised beaches result from changes in land-level. The great weight of ice during the Ice Age pushed parts of the continents down. As the ice melted, the sea-level rose quickly, but the land-level rose more slowly.

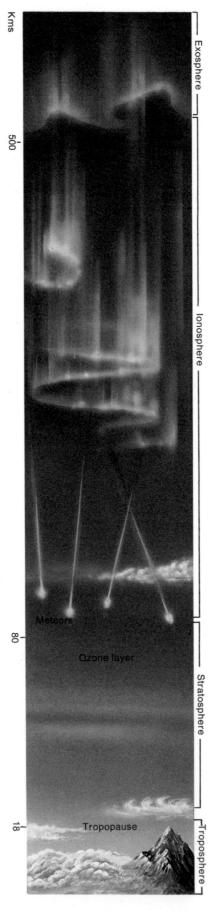

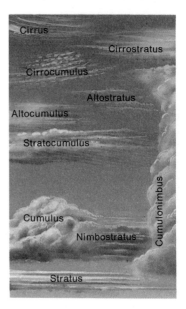

### ▶ WHAT IS THE ATMOS-PHERE MADE OF?

**The atmosphere is the air which surrounds the planet Earth. The gases in the air allow plants, animals and humans to live. The dampness and movement of the air near the Earth cause our weather. The atmosphere also shields us from the Sun's harmful rays and from falling meteorites.**

Air is made up of many gases. The most common are nitrogen (78%) and oxygen (21%). There are small amounts of other gases, including argon, water vapour and carbon dioxide.

The atmosphere is held round the Earth by gravity. Its pressure, temperature and composition vary according to the distance away from the Earth's surface. It can be divided into four layers.

The troposphere is about 18 kilometres thick over the Equator and about 8 kilometres thick over the Poles. It has 80% of the Earth's atmosphere. Air pressure, temperature and humidity (dampness) are greatest near the surface.

Above the troposphere is the stratosphere which reaches to 80 kilometres above the surface. The ozone layer filters out some of the Sun's harmful ultraviolet rays.

Beyond the stratosphere is the ionosphere. It helps to transmit radio waves, and meteoroids burn up in its layers.

About 500 kilometres above the earth's surface comes the exosphere. This has very little air and merges into outer space.

### ▲ WHAT KINDS OF CLOUDS CAN WE SEE?

**Clouds are made of millions of tiny water droplets or ice crystals suspended in the air. They are named according to their shape and height.**

Air cools when it rises. When air rises slowly over a large area, layers (strata) of clouds form. Cirrostratus is a thin, almost transparent layer of cloud at a high level. Altostratus is a thicker layer of cloud at high level. Nimbostratus forms at a lower level, while stratus clouds are layers within 500 metres of the Earth's surface.

When air rises rapidly, it produces puffy clouds. These are called cumulus clouds. At a high level they are called altocumulus. When they join together they form strato-cumulus. Cumulonimbus are great, towering thunder clouds.

A third type of cloud is cirrus, wisps of cloud high in the sky. Because of their shape, they are sometimes nick-named 'mares' tails'.

## ▲ WHAT IS THE DIFFER-ENCE BETWEEN A HURRI-CANE AND A TORNADO?

**Hurricanes and tornadoes are violent storms with whirling winds. A tornado covers a much smaller area than a hurricane, but it is often more violent.**

The huge swirling mass of cloud which rotates round the calm 'eye' of a hurricane may be over 400 kilometres across. The spiralling winds may reach 15 to 20 kilometres up into the atmosphere. Hurricanes form over warm oceans and gradually die out when they reach land.

A tornado is a violent twisting funnel of cloud which extends down to land from a large storm cloud. It may be only 50 to 500 metres wide, but it rushes across land at speeds of 30 to 65 kilometres an hour.

Winds in a tornado can be even more violent than in a hurricane. They twist up the funnel at speeds up to 650 kilometres an hour and cause a trail of damage along the tornado's narrow path.

## ▼ WHAT DO 'HIGH' AND 'LOW' MEAN ON A WEATHER MAP?

**Air pressure varies at different parts of the Earth's surface. Areas of high air pressure are marked 'high' on weather maps. Areas of low air pressure are marked 'low'. Air, like water, can flow and it is a rule that winds always blow from high to low.**

Areas of high pressure are sometimes called 'anti-cyclones'. Air presses down and flows gently outwards from an anticyclone. Such 'highs' often indicate clear skies and fine, dry weather. But anticyclones can also bring foggy weather.

Winds blow into areas of low pressure, which are sometimes called 'depressions'. 'Lows' usually indicate unsettled weather with wind and rain. Deep depressions, with very low pressure, usually bring gales and storms and very high tides.

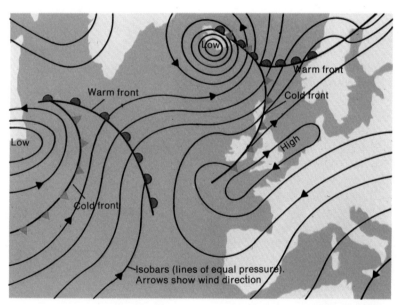

Isobars (lines of equal pressure).
Arrows show wind direction

## ▲ WHAT ARE 'FRONTS' ON WEATHER MAPS?

**A 'front' is the dividing line between two different kinds of air. The different kinds of air will not mix easily, and usually one kind of air is pushing over or under the other.**

'Fronts' are often found on weather maps of Western Europe because this area has varied types of air. Polar air pushing down from the north is cold. Some is cold and damp, some is cold and dry.

Tropical air pushing up from the south may be warm and moist, or warm and dry.

A body of air with similar temperatures and humidity (dampness) is called an air mass. The dividing line between two air masses is called a 'front'. A 'warm front' is where warm air is advancing. It rises over the colder air. A 'cold front' is where cold air is advancing: it pushes under the warm air. So on each front the warm air is rising. It cools and condenses and the result is clouds and rain or snow.

### ▼ WHAT ARE JET STREAMS?

**Jet streams are strong winds which blow from west to east high above the Earth's surface. If high-flying aircraft are travelling eastwards, jet streams can enable them to travel faster.**

Jet streams encircle the Earth at 10 to 15 kilometres above the surface. They blow in definite zones at about 250 kilometres an hour.

Usually there are two jet streams in each hemisphere: the sub-tropical jet stream and, nearer the Poles, the polar-front jet stream. They are strongest in winter and early spring. Jet streams may be marked by a line of clouds, as shown in the photograph.

The position and strength of the jet streams affect the weather in a complex way. The polar-front jet stream influences the number and the route of the fronts which give much of Europe its varied weather. The movement of the sub-tropical jet stream influences the monsoon in Asia.

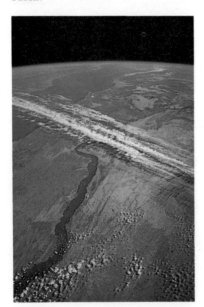

### ▼ WHAT IS THE MONSOON?

**'Monsoon' means season. This word is used for the season of heavy rain which occurs in some parts of the world, especially in southern and eastern Asia. This rainy season begins suddenly when winds from the sea sweep across the land.**

The maps show India, which has a monsoon climate. From April to June the weather gets hotter and hotter, and the air is very dry. Winds blow

Rainfall June–Oct
Winds in July

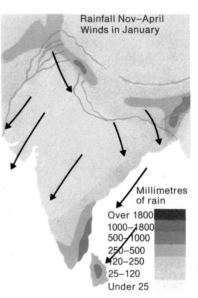
Rainfall Nov–April
Winds in January

Millimetres
of rain

Over 1800
1000–1800
500–1000
250–500
120–250
25–120
Under 25

### ▲ WHAT EFFECT DOES THE SEA HAVE ON CLIMATE?

**Winds blowing from sea to land usually bring moisture. Places near the sea have a less extreme climate than inland. Warm and cold ocean currents also affect the temperature of winds.**

Air blowing over a fairly warm sea quickly becomes saturated with moisture. If it rises and cools as it reaches land, much of the moisture will fall as rain near the coast.

outwards from the land.

In June or July, the monsoon bursts. The day when the rain will begin can be forecast. Then, winds begin to blow from the sea, bringing with them much-needed rain.

About 1700 millimetres of rain fall between June and September, and only another 100 millimetres in all the rest of the year. By September only a few showers fall in most parts of India. A pleasantly cool, dry season takes over. Once again, the winds blow from land to sea.

High land which faces winds from the sea has a very high rainfall.

Places near the sea are often cooler in summer than places inland. This is because the moving ocean absorbs the Sun's heat slowly in summer. But it is slow to lose its heat in winter, and the sea helps to keep coastal areas warmer than inland areas. Compare the average temperatures of London and Irkutsk, USSR, which are on almost the same latitude: London: January 4°C; July 18°C. Irkutsk: January −21°C; July 18°C.

## ▼ WHAT HAPPENS TO ALL THE WATER THAT FALLS TO EARTH?

**Rain or snow falls on to the land and flows off in rivers or glaciers, or soaks in as underground water. Eventually the water reaches the sea. Water is evaporated from the sea to form clouds, from which rain falls on to the Earth.**

This process is called the water cycle. Each part of the cycle depends on other parts, involving water as a liquid, a solid (ice) and a gas (water vapour).

Water is absorbed into the air over the land as well as the sea. It comes from lakes and rivers, wet soil and from plants. Water vapour condenses and returns to the land and sea in many different forms: dew, fog and hail, as well as rain and snow. Most falls over the sea, but about a quarter falls over land. Almost half that does reach the land evaporates soon after falling. The rest flows back to the sea. Water is constantly recycled in this way.

## ▲ WHAT IS SPECIAL ABOUT THE MEDITERRANEAN CLIMATE?

**Places near the Mediter-ranean Sea have hot, dry summers. Most of their rainfall comes in the warm winter months. This climate is the only one which has its rain at the coolest time of the year.**

A similar climate to the Mediterranean occurs in parts of California (USA), central Chile, south-west Australia and near Cape Town (South Africa).

All these places are on the west side of continents. In the winter they receive rain from westerly winds. All these areas are also close to deserts. In summer they share the high pressure found over deserts and have hot, dry weather. Plants native to these areas are adapted to survive long, hot droughts.

This change of season is caused by a shift in the world's wind pattern each year as the Sun is overhead at the Tropic of Cancer in June and the Tropic of Capricorn in December.

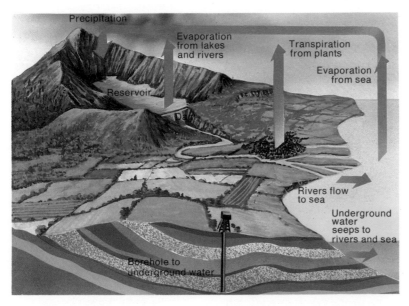

Precipitation

Evaporation from lakes and rivers

Transpiration from plants

Evaporation from sea

Reservoir

Dam

Rivers flow to sea

Underground water seeps to rivers and sea

Borehole to underground water

## ▲ WHERE DOES YOUR TAP WATER COME FROM?

**We break into the water cycle to obtain our water. Then we purify it and send it through pipes to our homes.**

Rainwater can be collected from the roof and stored in tanks. In some places water is pumped out of rivers or lakes and piped to homes. Else-where, the water we use comes from underground springs or boreholes. It is pumped up from permeable rocks such as chalk, limestone and sandstone in which water can collect.

But in most large cities there is not enough surface water or underground water for everyone. Water may be brought from other parts of the country where there is more rain or fewer people. Valleys in wet, hilly areas may be dammed for water storage. Near large towns, water may be stored in huge reservoirs.

In a few parts of the world, sea water is turned into fresh water (desalination), but this is a very expensive process.

Sea-level

### ▼ WHAT IS THE DIFFERENCE BETWEEN WEATHERING AND EROSION?

**'Weathering' is the breaking up of rocks by sun or frost, for example. 'Erosion' is the shaping of the Earth's surface by wind or water.**

When rocks are exposed to the atmosphere, they are affected by its temperature and moisture. 'Mechanical weathering' occurs when water in the rocks freezes and cracks the rocks. Constant heating and cooling splits the surface of some rocks, too.

'Chemical weathering' rots rocks. Rainwater reacts with some minerals to dissolve the rocks or change them chemically. Weathering may be speeded up by plant roots and burrowing animals.

Rock pieces broken by weathering are moved by rivers, glaciers, the sea or the wind. Wind and water erode most when they contain particles of rock. For instance, sand carried by desert winds may chisel rocks into strange shapes.

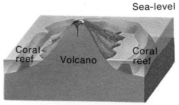

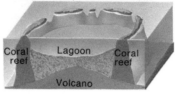

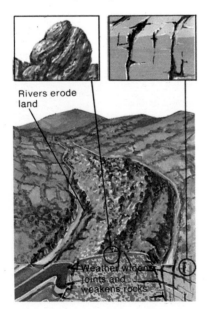

Rivers erode land

Weather widens joints and weakens rocks

### ▲ WHAT IS AN ATOLL?

**An atoll is a coral reef which forms an almost complete circle around a lagoon.**

The coral polyp is a tiny sea-creature which lives in a shell. New coral polyps grow on the shells of dead ones, eventually forming a great mass of coral. Corals live in fairly shallow water (up to 45 metres deep) that is warm (over 18°C) and clear. In ideal conditions large coral reefs may form.

The circular coral reefs of most atolls reach deep down into water where no coral can grow. As the diagrams show, they may once have been reefs in shallow water surrounding a volcano. As the island sinks, or the sea-level changes, the coral continues to grow. The original island disappears far below the lagoon, and the reef forms an atoll.

There are many atolls in the Pacific and Indian Oceans, where conditions are ideal for corals to flourish. Volcanic islands, some with coral reefs, are also found today.

### ▲ WHAT ARE STALACTITES AND STALAGMITES?

**Both these features are found in limestone caves. They are formed from a rock which is sometimes called 'dripstone'. Stalactites are columns of dripstone hanging down from the ceiling. Stalagmites rise from the floor.**

The word 'dripstone' gives a clue to the formation of stalactites and stalagmites.

Limestone is mainly made of calcium carbonate. When rainwater seeps through cracks in this rock it reacts with the calcium carbonate and gradually dissolves it. So water dripping from a cave roof is saturated with calcium carbonate and other minerals. As each drip hangs for a while, some water is evaporated, leaving a tiny deposit of calcium carbonate on the cave roof. Very slowly, these deposits grow to form stalactites.

Drips reaching the floor of the cave gradually form stalagmites. Natural pillars occur when stalactites and stalagmites join.

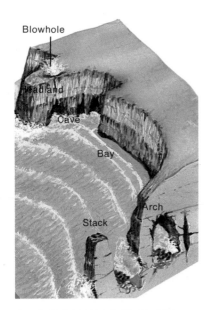

**In a desert, the sand grains are blown about and keep knocking each other. So they become rounded. In rivers and the sea, sand grains do not collide so often, so they are less rounded.**

Sand mainly consists of grains of quartz, but other minerals may be present. All these minerals have been weathered out of rocks.

When handfuls of desert sand and of beach sand are studied under the microscope, they look different. Sand grains from the desert (bottom) are mostly quartz. River and sea sand (top) often include softer minerals such as mica.

The rounded desert sand grains are all about the same size and look 'frosted' instead of shiny after countless collisions with each other in the wind. Sand grains in rivers and the sea have been 'cushioned' by water and are more varied in shape and size.

## ▲ WHAT HAPPENS WHEN THE SEA ATTACKS THE BASE OF A CLIFF?

**Great waves hurling water and stones at a cliff are an awesome sight. The sea undercuts cliffs, causing cliff falls and features such as caves, arches, bays and headlands.**

The effects of the sea's action differ according to the geology of the coast. Soft rocks wear away more quickly than hard rocks. The dip of the strata (rock layers) helps or hinders erosion. Faults and folds create weaknesses which the sea attacks.

Often, a notch can be seen in a cliff near high-tide level where the sea has battered the cliff. As this notch deepens, the cliff above will fall. The sea carves out bays in areas of weak rocks. Harder rocks are left extending out as headlands.

Cracks in even the hardest rocks are widened and deepened and may become caves. In a headland, caves may meet to form an arch. When an arch collapses, part of it is left as a stack.

## ▲ HOW IS NEW LAND CREATED BY THE SEA?

**The sea can build as well as destroy. When conditions are right, the sea can build sand dunes. Mud may collect on the sheltered side of sand and shingle ridges. Marshes grow and gradually new land develops.**

The sea can create areas of dunes. Sand pushed up a beach may be blown into sand dunes. Long-rooted grasses start to grow and 'fix' the dunes. More and more plants grow, creating an area of sand hills.

Tides and currents can move sand or shingle along a beach. Sometimes sand or shingle spits are formed. Water protected by such features is quite still, and sediments in the water sink to the bottom.

Gradually the water gets shallower, and more and more mud is exposed at low tide. Salt-loving marsh plants start to grow and trap more mud. Muddy creeks develop, channelling the outgoing tide.

▼ WHAT IS AN AVALANCHE?

**An avalanche is a mass of snow which comes loose from a mountainside and hurtles down a steep slope towards the valley below.**

Avalanches occur wherever there are high mountains, open slopes and heavy snow. Many avalanches occur each winter, but only a small number cause death and destruction. Avalanches vary in type. Some are formed of loose snow, and others consist of huge snow-slabs.

Changes of temperature and wind can cause avalanches. Changes in the depth, pressure and humidity of the snow itself can allow one layer to slide over another. Late winter is the worst time for avalanches, when there is plenty of snow but warmer weather starts a thaw.

Sometimes explosives are used to make small avalanches which prevent larger ones. Walls, snow-fences and snow-bridges are built on hillsides to break up avalanches. Planting trees on slopes helps to keep the snow stable.

▼ IN WHAT WAYS DO RIVERS CHANGE THE SHAPE OF THE LAND?

**Rivers can erode the land and deposit eroded material further down-stream.**

In the upper part of its course, the river flows down steep slopes. Rocks are bounced along by the water and help to erode the river bed. A deep V-shaped valley is formed.

On the lower land, the river meanders. Powerful river currents undercut the outside of the meanders and deposit sand and mud on the inside of meanders. This widens the valley.

At times of flood the river can cause great damage to low-lying land, and its course may be straightened. Old meanders are cut off to form oxbow lakes.

Near its mouth, the river flows over a broad flood-plain, where it deposits eroded material. If the river flows into a lake or sea with little or no tide then its silt is dumped to form a delta.

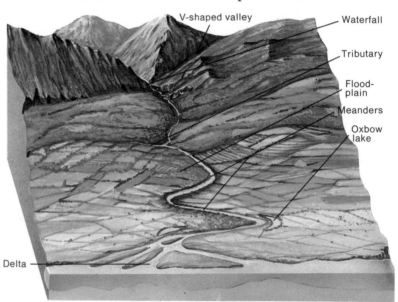

V-shaped valley · Waterfall · Tributary · Flood-plain · Meanders · Oxbow lake · Delta

▲ WHAT CAUSES FLOODS?

**Heavy and prolonged rain can flood large areas. Many parts of the world receive almost all their rain from heavy storms during a short wet season.**

The rocks of an area may help to cause floods. Impermeable rocks and large built-up areas cause the rain to run off the land very quickly. Streams and rivers may overflow and flood the surrounding land. Permeable rocks soak up the water.

When snow that has collected through the winter suddenly melts, there can be widespread flooding. Parts of Siberia are flooded every spring when the snow in the south melts while the mouths of the north-flowing rivers are still blocked by ice.

Very high tides can flood land, especially if there are strong winds. The low-lying country of Bangladesh suffers terrible floods when cyclones (hurricanes) cause exceptionally high tides.

## ▼ WHAT HAPPENED DURING THE ICE AGE?

**During the last million years, large parts of northern Europe and North America have been covered by ice. There was not just one cold period when the ice sheets advanced; there were many.**

The periods of ice advances are called 'glacials'. Snow accumulated, and glaciers and ice sheets extended over large areas. As these advanced, land was eroded and the sea-level was lower. There was much more sea ice and more icebergs than now.

In the interglacials much of the ice melted. Moraine and other glacial deposits were dumped over large areas. Melt-water left spreads of sand and gravel. The courses of rivers were often altered. Sea-level changed, flooding large areas.

Elsewhere in the world the pattern of ocean currents, winds and climate also changed with each glacial and interglacial.

## ▼ WHAT WOULD HAPPEN IF ALL THE WORLD'S ICE MELTED?

**If all the ice in the world melted, new land would be revealed in the Arctic and Antarctic and in some high mountains. But large areas of the world would be flooded as sea-level rose.**

Sea-level has changed in the past during glacials and interglacials, so it may change in the future. The depth of ice in parts of Greenland and Antarctica has now been measured, so scientists can estimate the amount of water stored there.

If all the world's ice melted, sea-level would rise by at least 65 metres. The coastline of Europe would change dramatically. Areas of low land would be flooded, including the whole of Denmark and the Netherlands. Many major cities would be drowned, including great capitals such as London, Dublin, Paris, Rome and Helsinki.

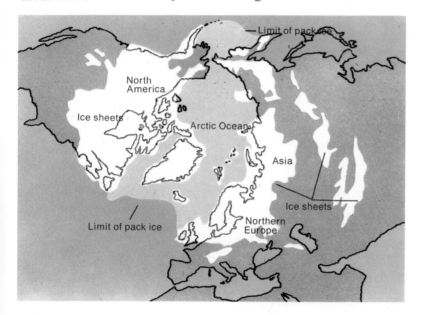

## ▲ WHAT ARE THE CHANCES OF ANOTHER ICE AGE?

**No one knows, partly because scientists still do not understand why an Ice Age begins.**

Some geologists point out that, in the past, the warm interglacials lasted about 10,000 years, and our climate has been as warm for that long already. Some climatologists say that the Earth's warmth is about the same now as 90,000 years ago when a sudden cooling probably occurred.

Historians know that Europe's climate has varied. Northern Europe was warmer and less stormy in Roman and Viking times. Between 1550 and 1880 there was a 'Little Ice Age' when winters were colder than they are now.

Some ecologists believe humans could create an Ice Age. All the dust and fumes we add to the air could reduce the Sun's heat. Others argue that as we burn so much fuel, and chop down forests, we increase the carbon dioxide in the air. This could trap more of the Sun's heat.

# THE PAST

### ▼ WHAT WAS AUSTRALOPITHECUS?

**About four million years ago, a man-like ape lived in Africa. Its name, *Australopithecus*, means 'southern ape'. Skulls and other bones have been discovered and they tell us something about its life.**

From its remains, scientists know that Australopithecus walked on two legs, like us. Its brain was only a third the size of ours, yet it used stone tools.

Australopithecus probably died out before modern humans appeared. It was not our ancestor, for it seems that both Australopithecus and ourselves are descended from an even older ape-like creature.

There were two types of Australopithecus. One was more heavily built than the other.

### ▼ WHAT IS ARCHAEOLOGY?

**Archaeology is the study of the past. The first archaeologists were treasure-hunters, interested only in gold and jewels. Modern archaeologists are patient scientists.**

Every object, no matter how ordinary, is part of history. So an archaeologist is just as interested in a broken pot as in a gold crown.

Some famous finds in archaeology are the Palace at Knossos in Crete (1899), the tomb of the Egyptian pharaoh Tutankhamun (1922), and the tomb of the Chinese emperor Qin Shihuangdi (1979).

Clues to the past are often hidden. A photograph from the air, for example, can show the outline of a building long since buried beneath fields.

### ▼ WHAT HAPPENS AT AN ARCHAEOLOGICAL 'DIG'?

**To uncover the past, archaeologists must often excavate, or dig, below ground. Valuable finds may lie buried beneath centuries of soil, or more recent buildings.**

Archaeologists may have to work fast (if they are on a building site, for instance). Yet every object, no matter how small, is a clue to the past. It must be patiently removed, cleaned and labelled. Its position is recorded so that a picture of the whole site is built up.

The deeper the dig, the older will be the remains. With the aid of science, we can now tell the age of a bone or a fragment of pottery fairly accurately. An expert can learn a great deal even from a rubbish pit.

**Millions of years ago the first people picked up pebbles to use as tools. This was the beginning of the Stone Age. Tool-using was a great advance in our history.**

The early 'hominids', or ape-people, walked upright. This left their hands free to use tools. At first they just picked up stones of a useful shape. But in time they learned how to make flint tools with sharp cutting edges.

More advanced, and more like us, were *Homo erectus* ('upright man') and *Homo sapiens* ('wise man'). About 35,000 years ago people very like ourselves had appeared. They lived in rough shelters and caves, and hunted animals for food.

These people made tools and weapons, and used fire. Fire and stone weapons, such as knives and spears, gave humans power over much larger and stronger animals.

The Stone Age ended only when people learned how to use metals – first copper and bronze, and then iron. Some people, such as the Australian Aboriginals, went on using stone tools into modern times.

Great skill is needed to make good stone tools. Some early people may have been better than others at tool-making. So they became the first experts, making tools for the rest of the tribe. In turn, this may have led to the beginning of trade, as tool-makers exchanged tools for food or animal skins.

### ▲ WHAT WAS FOUND IN THE LASCAUX CAVES?

**Lascaux is the name of a cave system in the Dordogne region of France. In 1940 four boys went into the caves, looking for a dog. They were startled to see paintings of animals on the walls of a great cavern. We now know that these cave paintings were made about 17,000 years ago.**

The Lascaux caves are full of wonderfully life-like and colourful paintings. They show the animals that the artists knew and hunted, such as cattle, horses and rhinoceroses. There were also remains in the caves of the people who worked there, including oil lamps and paints used by the artists.

We know little about the people who made the cave paintings. They were probably hunters and may have used the cave as a religious centre. In 1963 the caves were closed because the paintings were starting to fade.

### ▼ WHAT WAS A ZIGGURAT?

**The people of ancient Mesopotamia, in the Middle East, built huge temples called ziggurats. A ziggurat was pyramid-shaped, with four stepped sides. Between 4000 and 2500 years ago many great ziggurats were built.**

Ziggurats were always built of brick. Unlike pyramids (which were tombs), ziggurats had no internal chambers. To reach the top, the people walked up a stairway or a ramp on the outside. But experts cannot work out how people reached the top of some ziggurats because no stairs or ramps remain.

The largest ziggurat is 100 metres square and was originally about 50 metres high. The shrine of the god was at the very top, in a special court, or room.

The Hanging Gardens of Babylon, one of the wonders of the ancient world, were built like a ziggurat. The sides and terraces were planted with trees and flowering plants.

### ▲ WHAT ARE HIEROGLYPHICS?

**The ancient Egyptians used a complicated kind of sign-writing. The Greeks called these signs 'hieroglyphs' (sacred writing). For centuries, experts puzzled over the meaning of the hieroglyphs on temples and tombs.**

Hieroglyphics was a more advanced version of the picture-writing the Egyptians first used. Only priests and scribes could master it, and inscriptions were written on the walls of buildings.

No one could read this ancient script until 1799, when a tablet, called the Rosetta Stone, was discovered. It had the same inscription in three forms of writing: hieroglyphics, Coptic Egyptian and Greek. Because the last two were understood, it was possible to decipher the hieroglyphs. This was done by a French scholar called Jean-François Champollion, and it was the key to many of the secrets of ancient Egypt.

### ▲ WHAT IS THE SPHINX?

**At Giza in Egypt stands a colossal statue. It has a lion's body, but the head of a man. This is the Sphinx, some 4500 years old, and one of the most famous monuments in the world.**

The word *sphinx* is Greek. In Greek legend, the sphinx was a monster which asked a riddle and devoured those who failed to answer the riddle correctly.

The Sphinx at Giza was built during the reign of the Egyptian king Khafre. The Sphinx's face is a portrait of the king. The figure is 80 metres long and over 20 metres high. Walls round the Sphinx protect it from the drifting sands.

All Egyptian sphinxes are shown with men's heads. But in other parts of the ancient world, sphinxes were often given women's heads.

Sometimes rows of sphinxes were set up to stand guard over palaces or royal tombs. These sphinxes were often shown with wings and a lion's body.

## ▲ WHAT WAS THE ORACLE AT DELPHI?

**The ancient Greeks believed that the gods could speak to people on Earth. The Oracle at Delphi was thought to be such a place. It was said to mark the centre of the world.**

From a crack in the rock at Delphi came magical vapours, giving the power of prophecy. Within the crack lived the serpent, Python, guardian of the Oracle. Python was slain by Apollo, god of the Sun, and a temple sacred to Apollo was built at Delphi.

This story drew visitors to Delphi from far and wide. They climbed the sacred path to the temple, and handed their questions to the priests. The high-priestess, Pythia, was the voice of the Oracle. Sitting on a tripod above the crack, she spoke while in a trance. Her replies were in a strange language, and were interpreted by the priests.

The Oracle was abolished by the Romans in AD 399, after it had foretold its own doom.

## ▲ WHAT WAS THE ACROPOLIS?

**Above the Greek city of Athens stands the hilltop site of the Acropolis. Among its temples and shrines is the Parthenon.**

The word *acropolis* comes from two Greek words meaning 'high city'. In ancient times, many cities had an acropolis, or stronghold, on a hill.

The Acropolis at Athens was ringed by a wall and had nine gates. When it was rebuilt in the 5th century BC, it must have looked even more beautiful than it is today, for its fine buildings were made of white marble.

The first kings of Athens built their palaces on the Acropolis. Later, it became the centre of Athenian life.

Today, the ruins on the Acropolis remind us of the splendour of Greek civilization. But they are almost too popular with tourists, whose footsteps threaten to wear away the ancient rocks.

## ▼ WHAT WAS THE COLOSSEUM BUILT FOR?

**The Colosseum was a huge stadium in ancient Rome. Crowds flocked there to see the 'games', at which there were fights and other bloody contests.**

Inside stadiums like the Colosseum, audiences of 20,000 or more could sit in tiers around the arena. The contests took place in the arena, which was like a circus ring. The arena could even be flooded to stage mock sea-battles!

Romans liked cruel sports. Animals were matched against men or other animals. Specially trained fighters, known as gladiators, fought to the death. Some gladiators, called *retiarii*, were armed with a net and a trident (a three-pronged stabbing fork). Other gladiators fought with swords, spears and lassos.

The Emperor often presided at the games. People demanded more and more lavish shows. Sometimes thousands of wild beasts and people were killed in the arena during one season.

### ▶ WHAT WAS A SAMURAI?

**The samurai were the knights of medieval Japan. They were proud and brave, and would fight to the death for their lord. The samurai's fantastic armour struck fear into their foes.**

During the Middle Ages, Japan was torn by civil war. During this time, samurai formed an army of highly-trained warriors. They fought on horseback and their favourite weapons were long swords. They were also expert bowmen.

The samurai despised cowards. They would never surrender. When gunpowder muskets first appeared, they called them 'cowards' weapons'. Yet, in the end, it was musket fire that defeated the samurai with their swords and armour.

For 800 years the samurai held on to their special place in Japanese life. Even when they were no longer required in battle, they remained powerful as the upholders of Japan's ancient customs.

### ◀ WHAT WAS A KNIGHT?

**In the Middle Ages, knights were specially trained soldiers. They wore armour and fought on horseback. A knight swore an oath to serve his king. In return, the king gave land to the knight.**

The king needed loyal warriors to fight his wars and also to help him rule the land. His knights were the pride of his army. In return for their service, the knights received payment in the form of lands. This arrangement, called feudalism, lasted for hundreds of years.

Some knights were 'dubbed' (made a knight) on the field of battle. But most trained from boyhood, serving first as a page and then as a squire to an older knight.

Knights were supposed to uphold the law, and be honourable. So the idea of a special knightly code of honour arose. This was called 'chivalry'.

The most famous knights were the legendary Knights of the Round Table.

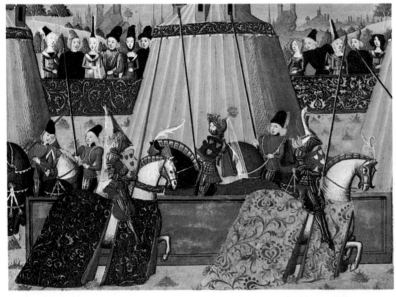

### ▲ WHAT WAS A JOUSTING TOURNAMENT?

**To train for battle, and to show off their skill, knights took part in mock fights. These were known as jousts. Such contests took place in front of an audience at open-air tournaments. Jousting often took place at celebrations such as coronations.**

Jousting was a mock fight between two knights. They fought in an enclosure known as the 'lists'. The knights wore armour and rode horses. They charged at one another, trying to knock each other off their horses with lances. The fight often continued on foot, with the knights using swords and clubs.

At a tournament, crowds gathered to watch jousts and other mock battles. Sometimes the knights fought so fiercely that they killed or wounded one another. So special rules were introduced to make jousting safer, and the knights had to use blunt weapons.

## ◀ WHAT WAS THE RENAISSANCE?

**The word *Renaissance* means 'rebirth'. It describes the time in Europe's history when people rediscovered the art and learning of the past, and added new, exciting ideas of their own.**

After the fall of the Roman Empire (about AD 500), much of the ancient learning was forgotten. During the Middle Ages, learning was closely tied to religion. Few people could read or write.

Around 1500, new ideas began to emerge. Artists such as Leonardo da Vinci looked back to ancient Greece and Rome for inspiration. Scientists, such as Copernicus, studied the world and disagreed with the teachings of the Church about it. The time was ripe for change. There were wealthy merchants ready to back new ventures. Also, there were new ways of spreading knowledge, such as Gutenberg's newly-invented printing press.

## ▶ WHAT WAS THE NEW WORLD?

**To Europeans of the 1400s, 'the world' meant Europe, Africa and Asia. But as European sailors began to venture farther from home, they discovered a New World – the continent of America.**

Viking rovers actually landed in North America around AD 1000. But almost 500 years passed before the next European explorers arrived. Ships were small and clumsy and sailors feared to sail out of sight of land. They had no compasses or maps.

In 1453 the Turks captured Constantinople. This stopped European merchants reaching Asia overland. So they set out to find a new sea route to the East. When Christopher Columbus left Spain in 1492, he hoped to find a westerly passage to the rich spice islands of the Indies.

Columbus believed that the world was round. But he did not imagine that beyond the Atlantic Ocean he would land on the shores of a New World, the vast continent of America.

## ▲ WHAT WAS THE SLAVE TRADE?

**Slavery is an ancient and evil trade. The ancient Greeks and Egyptians, for example, made slaves of people captured in war. After Europeans settled in America, slaves captured in Africa were shipped across the sea to work in the American plantations.**

The Arabs had traded in African slaves for centuries before Europeans joined in during the 1500s. Slave ships from Africa crossed the Atlantic Ocean, packed with men, women and children.

Many slaves died during the dreadful voyages. In America the slaves were sold in slave markets. Some worked as house servants, but most worked on cotton and sugar plantations. Many were ill-treated by their masters. Britain eventually banned the slave trade in 1807. But the black slaves in the southern United States did not gain their freedom until the American Civil War of 1861–65.

### ▼ WHAT WAS THE INDUSTRIAL REVOLUTION?

**In history, a revolution is a time of great change. In the late 1700s and early 1800s, a new age began – the Age of Machines. It was also the Age of Industry, when millions of people began to work in mills, mines and factories.**

Improved transport made these changes possible. Canals and railways carried goods from the new factories to the ports. Inside the

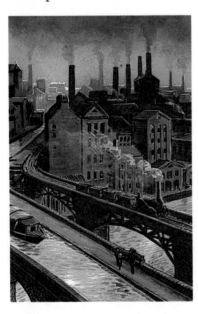

factories, the steam engine's mighty power was harnessed to drive machinery. Coal was the fuel, iron was the material and steam was the power that made the Industrial Revolution.

The new railways carried people faster than ever before. New iron ships steamed the oceans. Within a few years villages grew into towns.

The Industrial Revolution made Europe and America rich and powerful. Factory owners made fortunes. But factory workers often had to live in overcrowded slums.

### ▼ WHAT CAUSED WORLD WAR I?

**The Great War of 1914–18 was the most terrible the world had seen. Many nations took part, and millions of people died. The war was caused by rivalry in Europe. But it actually began with a murder.**

In 1914 the Austrian Archduke Ferdinand was shot dead by a rebel while visiting Sarajevo in Serbia (now part of Yugoslavia). This murder started a chain of events that led to war in Europe within two months.

On one side were Germany, Austria and Turkey. On the other were Britain, France and Russia, joined later by the USA. Most people thought the war would end quickly. But new weapons, such as the machine gun, were so deadly that neither side could break through. Armies became bogged down in trench warfare. For the first time ever, civilians were bombed from the air. The war dragged on until 1918, when Germany surrendered.

### ▼ WHAT WAS THE WALL STREET CRASH?

**In the 1930s the world was swept into a disastrous money crisis. Money lost its value. Businesses collapsed and trade slumped. The crisis began on Wall Street, in New York.**

Wall Street was the home of the US Stock Market, where stocks and shares were traded. In October 1929 the market 'crashed'.

Before the collapse, people

had been buying shares recklessly. Prices rose high above their true value. Suddenly, a panic began, and everyone started selling.

Banks were ruined. Many businesses and factories closed. The Wall Street Crash brought on the Great Depression – a slump in world trade which lasted for several years. Millions of people lost their jobs during the slump. Soup kitchens, like the one shown in the photograph, were set up to provide food for unemployed people.

## ▼ WHAT IS NATO?

**'NATO' stands for North Atlantic Treaty Organization. It is a military alliance set up in 1949 by the USA and its allies in Western Europe. Its headquarters are in Brussels, Belgium.**

When World War II ended, Europe was in ruins. It was also divided in two, for the eastern half was controlled by the USSR. The Western European nations feared that the USSR might try to attack them, so they set up an alliance for self-defence.

The USA and Canada are also members of the North Atlantic Treaty Organization. NATO now has 15 members.

NATO has its own commander, and each country contributes part of its armed forces. Troops, aircraft and ships of NATO carry out manoeuvres together to develop co-operation between the nations.

The countries of Eastern Europe belong to a similar alliance. This is known as the Warsaw Pact.

**Map of Europe**

NATO countries

Warsaw Pact countries

Iceland
Norway
United Kingdom
Denmark
Netherlands
Belgium
Luxembourg
West Germany
France
Portugal
Italy
USSR
Poland
East Germany
Czechoslovakia
Hungary
Romania
Bulgaria
Turkey
Greece

## ▲ WHAT IS THE 'COLD WAR'?

**World War II ended in 1945, but the victorious Allies were soon quarrelling. The USA and the USSR were suspicious of one another. They began an 'arms race' and disagreed on many things. This is the so-called 'cold war'.**

In 1945 Europe was divided by the 'iron curtain', separating the Communist East from the non-Communist West. The USSR set up Communist governments in the countries it had freed from Nazi rule.

The struggle between the West (or 'Free World') and the East (Communists) went on in many parts of the world. The Korean War (1950–53) became a trial of strength between the two sides. So, too, was the Vietnam War (1945–76). Today, the same mistrust that began the cold war threatens the world with destruction, because of the build-up of nuclear weapons on both sides.

## ▼ WHAT IS THE 'THIRD WORLD'?

**The world can be divided into three, according to economic and political differences. One part is made up of wealthy countries such as the USA. Another is made up of communist countries such as the USSR and China. The Third World is made up of poor, less developed countries with few natural resources.**

Most Third World countries are in Africa and Asia. When the United Nations was set up in 1945, one of its aims was to help poor countries. Many of these countries were then colonies, ruled by Europeans. Today, almost all are independent.

Few Third World countries can grow enough food to feed their growing populations or earn enough money by trade to build homes, schools and hospitals quickly enough.

Some help for the Third World comes from UN experts, who can advise on new farming methods and train people in new skills.

# HOW PEOPLE LIVE

### ▼ WHAT IS A MERMAID?

**Mermaids were mythical beasts said to live in the sea. The upper half of a mermaid's body was that of a woman but the lower half was that of a fish, with scales and a tail.**

Many people believed that mermaids were as real as any other animal. They were said to love singing and to have magic powers.

People thought mermaids were usually dangerous, and used their beautiful voices to lure sailors to death by drowning. But many tales tell of men who gained power over a mermaid by stealing her mirror or comb, and then married her and took her to live on dry land.

Some people have mistaken a distant seal or sea cow for a mermaid. Maybe this is how the idea of mermaids began.

### ▼ WHAT IS A UNICORN?

**The unicorn was a mythical beast said to look like a horse. It had a long, straight, spiral horn jutting from its forehead.**

In Greek and Roman myths, the unicorn had hind legs like

an antelope's and a tail like that of a lion. The body was white, the head was red, and the eyes were blue. The horn had a white base, black middle and red tip.

In the Middle Ages the unicorn stood for purity. Christian artists often pictured a unicorn with holy people like the Virgin Mary.

Zoologists think that the idea of the unicorn arose when someone saw an oryx far off. From a distance, this big desert antelope sometimes seems to have one long horn instead of two horns.

### ▼ WHAT IS A DRAGON?

**Dragons are mythical beasts. Many were supposed to have a snake's body and a bat's wings. They breathed fire.**

In fact different people had different notions of what

dragons looked like. To the ancient Greeks a dragon was a huge snake. Chinese dragons had legs with clawed feet, but no wings.

Greeks and Romans believed that dragons could be wise and good, but Jews and Christians always thought dragons were evil and dangerous. A Christian legend tells how St George used a magic sword to kill a dragon about to eat a princess.

The Komodo dragons that live on a few Indonesian islands are really no more than very large lizards.

## ▼ WHAT IS A FLYING SAUCER?

**'Flying saucer' is a name often used for any kind of strange object seen in the sky. People also describe such objects as unidentified flying objects, or UFOs for short.**

Flying saucers got their name because many were supposed to look like giant saucers. Thousands have been sighted around the world. Many stood still; others dashed across the sky faster than a

plane. This has led some people to think that flying saucers are spaceships from other worlds.

Scientists have rather less exciting explanations. They have found that most flying saucers were really ordinary objects such as weather balloons, planets, meteors or aircraft seen in unusual light.

A few people claim they actually watched a flying saucer land, and met strange beings who came out of it. But doctors usually find that all this happened only in the watcher's own imagination.

## ▼ WHAT IS THE LOCH NESS MONSTER?

**This is supposed to be a huge water animal. It is said to live in northern Scotland in a long, deep lake called Loch Ness.**

Many visitors to Loch Ness say they have seen the monster rising from the lake. Some have even photographed objects that might be parts of it. The photographs seem to show a beast about nine metres long. It appears to have a long,

snaky neck, a big barrel-shaped body, and flippers.

Giant reptiles like this once swam in many seas; they are known as plesiosaurs. But all are thought to have died out 65 million years ago.

Many people who thought they saw the monster may have been mistaken. Otters, fish, and even waves, sometimes look like a strange, large animal.

Boats with echo-sounders have shown something large that moves deep down in the lake. Perhaps Loch Ness *does* have a prehistoric monster.

## ▲ WHAT WAS THE MINOTAUR?

**The Minotaur was a mythical monster with a bull's head and a man's body. It was supposed to live on the island of Crete in the Mediterranean Sea.**

Greek legend tells that the Minotaur was the child of a white bull and the queen of Crete. The Cretan king, Minos, kept the beast in the Labyrinth. This building was shaped as a maze, from which no one could find the way out. Each year seven youths and seven maidens from the Greek city of Athens were put in the Labyrinth for the bull-man to eat.

One year, an Athenian prince called Theseus killed the Minotaur. Theseus then escaped from the Labyrinth by following a thread given to him by Ariadne, the daughter of the Cretan king.

Archaeologists have dug up ancient palace ruins on Crete. They found many corridors and wall paintings of people playing daring games with bulls. Perhaps these led to the Minotaur legend.

## ▲ WHAT IS A SYNAGOGUE?

**A synagogue is a Jewish place of worship and learning. The word means 'to bring together'. Judaists (people belonging to the religion of Judaism) have been meeting in synagogues for more than two thousand years.**

Synagogues need not be built in any particular way, as most churches are. But all hold an ever-burning lamp, which stands for the everlasting faith of the Jewish people.

There is also a closet called the holy ark. This holds the Scrolls of the Law (the Jewish Scripture), read out to the worshippers. The services are led by a person who stands on a platform or *bimah*. Any Jew may do this, but most synagogues have a cantor who chants religious music and leads the people in prayer.

The person responsible for religious services and teaching is a rabbi. Rabbis are learned people, and their tasks include explaining the Jewish Scriptures.

## ▼ WHAT IS A MOSQUE?

**A mosque is a place of worship for Muslims. They believe in the faith called Islam. The word *mosque* comes from the Arabic for 'temple'.**

A mosque may be a room or a splendid group of large buildings. Many mosques have towers called minarets, from where *muezzins* or criers call people to worship at the hours of prayer.

Muslims remove their shoes and wash in a courtyard. Then they kneel facing a *mihrab* or prayer niche. This shows the direction of Mecca, the holiest city of Islam. Prayers are led by an *imam* who stands in a *mimbar*, or pulpit.

Early mosques were little more than fenced yards. Now many have a gleaming dome, graceful minarets, and a *maktab*, or school. Mosques are often decorated with beautiful patterns but there are no pictures of people or other living things. Islam forbids Muslims to copy what they believe God created.

## ▲ WHAT IS THE KORAN?

**This is the holy book of Islam. Its name means 'a recitation'. Muslims believe that the angel Gabriel told its words to the Prophet Muhammad before he died in AD 632.**

The Koran contains 114 *suras*, or chapters, made up of verses that rhyme and are written in Arabic. The world's hundreds of millions of Muslims believe these verses bring a message from Allah, as they call God.

The Koran says that Allah is the only God. It declares that God made the universe, and it calls on all people to submit to God's will. *Islam* means 'submission'.

The book tells how to lead a good daily life. People must pray every day, give to the poor and be brave, just and humble. The Koran says that one day all will come before God to be judged.

The Koran says that Abraham, Moses and Jesus were God's messengers, or prophets, and that the last prophet was Muhammad.

## ▼ WHAT IS A BUDDHIST?

**A Buddhist is a follower of Siddhartha Gautama, a long-dead Indian prince known by his title 'Buddha', which means 'Enlightened One'. There are over 200 million Buddhists.**

Buddhists believe people suffer because they want what they do not have. Buddhists think the way to escape sorrow is to free yourself from selfish desires.

Buddhists try to have the right beliefs and right hopes, say the right words, do the right things, live the right way of life, make the right effort, think the right thoughts and concentrate in the right way. They try not to be carried away by their feelings or do wrong, but to love their enemies.

Many become monks, living in monasteries and begging for food. All hope to understand their own inner lives and to reach perfect freedom of mind and peace. Buddhists call this condition *nirvana*.

## ▲ WHAT IS A PRAYER WHEEL?

**Prayer wheels are metal or wooden cylinders containing rolls of paper with printed prayers. They are used by some Buddhists, especially in Tibet.**

Each wheel is free to spin around on a rod. Some prayer wheels stand on a table, but others are held in the hand by a handle. When the hand makes a circling movement, a weight hung from the cylinder makes it revolve.

A prayer wheel may contain a number of prayers printed on the roll of paper which is placed inside the cylinder. Each time the wheel is turned, this is supposed to count as saying the prayer as many times as it is printed on the roll. In fact the prayers represent mystical sounds called *mantras*.

Mantras are part of a strange group of magical signs and sounds that found their way into Buddhism in Tibet.

## ▼ WHAT IS A BAR MITZVAH?

**This is a ceremony for Jewish boys. Its name means 'a son of the commandment'. The boys who take part are those thought old enough to obey the commandments of the Jewish religion.**

Before the ceremony, each boy receives special instruction in what he must learn and do. The bar mitzvah ceremony is held in a synagogue, usually on the Saturday after the boy's thirteenth birthday. He has to read from a scroll bearing the words of the Torah, the Jewish Law. Then he takes on the religious duties of an adult.

After the ceremony the boy's family invite friends and relatives to a feast. All give the boy presents. At one time boys used to make a speech to show that they knew the Bible and Jewish teachings.

To many Jewish families, the bar mitzvah is almost as important as a wedding. Many Jewish girls take part in a similar ceremony, called a *bas mitzvah*.

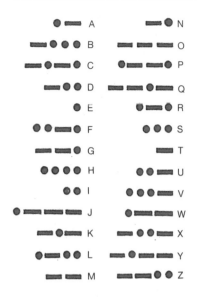

## ◄ WHAT IS MORSE CODE?

**This is a code using dots and dashes to stand for letters and numbers. It was once the main way of sending telegraph signals along wires or by radio. The code was invented in 1837 by the American inventor Samuel Morse.**

In Morse code, different letters, numbers and punctuation marks are given as different groups of dots and dashes. Dots are sent as short signals, dashes as long signals.

Signals are made by pressing the key of a sending device which alters a continuous electrical or radio signal and produces rapid sounds in a receiver.

The longer you press the key, the longer the signal. One dot lasts half as long as a short dash. A short dash lasts half as long as a long dash. Each gap between the dots and dashes making up a letter lasts as long as one dot. Each gap between the letters of a word lasts as long as three dots.

## ◄ WHAT IS SEMAPHORE USED FOR?

**Semaphore is a method of using flags or mechanical arms or lights to signal messages. Its name comes from two Greek words meaning 'signal carrier'.**

Semaphore signalling was invented as a way of sending signals between people who could see one another but were out of earshot. Sailors use semaphore to signal from ship to ship when they are afraid their radio signals might be overheard by an enemy.

A signaller holds two flags or lights at arm's length and moves his arms to different positions, like the hands on a clock. Each position stands for a different letter. To show numbers, the signaller gives a special numeral signal. This is followed by a letter of the alphabet corresponding to each number.

Semaphore markers on a railway line may form part of the points mechanism. They show train drivers how the points have been set.

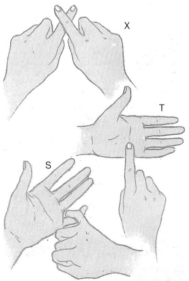

## ◄ WHAT IS DEAF-AND-DUMB LANGUAGE?

**Deaf-and-dumb language is a way of 'talking' with the fingers and hands instead of the mouth. People who are unable to speak or hear can use it to hold conversations.**

There are two main kinds of deaf-and-dumb sign language. One method uses one hand, the other uses both hands. In both methods, different finger positions stand for different letters of the alphabet. Each method involves spelling out words one letter at a time. Talking in deaf-and-dumb sign language is much slower than speaking. Deaf-and-dumb people can talk faster if they also use other gestures and facial expressions as short cuts.

Deaf-and-dumb language is used less than it once was. This is because people who are born deaf can now be taught to speak. Many deaf people also now use hearing aids or learn to lip-read spoken sound by watching the shapes of the speaker's lips.

## ▶ WHAT IS BRAILLE?

**Braille is a code of raised dots. Blind people can read Braille by running their fingers over the dots on a page. The code was invented in the 1820s by a blind French student called Louis Braille.**

Braille is based on a block of six dots which is two dots wide and three dots high. By leaving out different dots, Braille produced 63 different dot patterns standing for different letters, punctuation marks, numbers and even musical notes.

Ten patterns made from the top four dots stand for the first ten letters of the alphabet. Adding a special number sign turns each of these into a number. Adding a bottom left-hand dot to the patterns for A to J makes the letters K to T. Adding a bottom right-hand dot to the patterns for K to O makes the letters U to Z. Other groups of dots build simple words or sounds of speech. People can also type Braille with a special typewriter.

## ▶ WHAT IS ESPERANTO?

**Esperanto is a language invented to make it easy for people of all nations to understand one another. Esperanto was introduced in 1887 in a book written by its Polish inventor, Ludwik Zamenhof.**

The Esperanto alphabet uses letters from the Roman alphabet, but not Q, W, X or Y. Some letters have two sounds. The second sound is shown by a mark over the letter.

Esperanto words come mostly from words whose main parts are shared by important European languages. But all nouns end in 'o' and adjectives end in 'a'.

There are no muddling exceptions to the rules of grammar as there are in other languages. This makes Esperanto easy to study. People can learn to speak Esperanto up to twenty times faster than it takes them to learn to speak some other languages. The picture shows the first French taxi-driver to speak Esperanto.

## ▶ WHAT IS MICROFILM USED FOR?

*Micro* **means 'small'. Microfilm is used to store bulky information in a small space. It bears extremely tiny photographic copies of printed pages or other kinds of information.**

Microfilm is often used for making copies of books and newspapers, for use in schools or libraries. This adds enormously to the amount of information that can be kept.

Businesses store microfilm copies of business records that would otherwise take up too much office space.

A special camera is used to photograph each page of a book on a tiny panel on a roll of film. As many as a thousand pages can be stored on a microfiche – a sheet of microfilm no bigger than a person's hand.

To read the film, you place it in a machine (seen here) that greatly enlarges the words on the microfilm. To find a special panel on a strip of film you wind on the film.

### ▲ WHAT IS A SARI?

**This is a straight length of woven fabric worn by many Indian women. They drape it loosely around the entire body so that one end serves as a skirt and the other covers the shoulders or the head.**

Each sari measures from 5.5 to 8 metres long. A sari is the only piece of clothing that poorer women wear. Most other women wear one over a half-slip.

They wrap the lower end of the sari several times around the waist to form a full skirt with pleats at the front. Then they drape the upper end of the sari loosely over the chest or the shoulders. Usually they also wear a blouse or a rather similar upper garment called a *choli*.

Peasants who work in the fields often wear plain cloth saris coloured white or blue. But many wealthy Indian women have expensive saris of silk with borders of gold thread. Saris have been worn for thousands of years.

### ▲ WHAT IS A KIMONO USED FOR?

**The name *kimono* simply means a 'wearing thing'. Kimonos are loose robes worn by Japanese men and women, mostly indoors. The Japanese have been wearing clothes like this for hundreds of years.**

Each kimono, including its sleeves, is cut out of a single piece of material. This is shaped to make a loose robe with a flowing skirt and wide sleeves.

A kimono is usually worn with a sash called an *obi* tied around the waist. The kimono may be made of cotton or silk. Some of the most splendid ones are made of rich silk crêpe with embroidered patterns, and sashes of patterned brocade.

Kimonos are comfortable as well as beautiful. Many Japanese men and women wear light, simple cotton kimonos indoors. Dressy kimonos are very expensive and worn only on special occasions.

### ▲ WHAT IS A KILT?

**A kilt is a knee-length pleated skirt traditionally worn by men from the Scottish Highlands and Ireland. Nowadays they wear their kilts only on special occasions.**

Each kilt is pleated at the back from the waist, but the front is plain. Scottish kilts are made of tartans. These are woollen fabrics with usually a red or green background that is criss-crossed by stripes of various colours. Different patterns represent different Highland clans or districts. The traditional Irish kilts are a plain saffron colour.

Most patterned kilts have permanent pleats folded so that the pattern shows up when seen from any angle. Highland regiments have box-pleated kilts with one main stripe showing down each pleat. In front of the kilt, a Highlander may wear a *sporran*, a fur-covered pouch. The men of ancient Egypt wore white linen kilts.

### ▲ WHAT IS APARTHEID?

### ▲ WHAT ARE GUERRILLAS?

### ▲ WHAT ARE MERCENARIES?

**This Afrikaans word means 'apartness'. South Africa's white rulers used it to describe their policy for the separate development of the white and non-white peoples of South Africa.**

Strict apartheid laws keep whites and non-whites apart. Non-whites are forbidden to marry whites or do the same jobs or live in the same places as whites. Many blacks now live in tribal reserves, or their own nation-states.

South Africa's government said apartheid would help the non-whites to be better off by helping themselves. But many people feel that this cannot happen while most wealth and power belongs to the whites, who are far fewer than the blacks and coloureds.

By the 1980s, though, South Africa had relaxed certain apartheid rules. For instance, people of any colour became freer to watch or play some sports together. Also it became easier for blacks to work and travel in cities.

**Guerrillas are fighters who make hit-and-run raids on enemy forces during a war. They tend to fight in small groups, not as part of a main army, and might not wear uniforms. The word *guerrilla* is Spanish for 'little war'.**

Bands of guerrillas often fight behind enemy lines. They make sudden attacks against enemy outposts, ambush convoys of enemy lorries, or blow up enemy trains. Guerrillas often find food and hiding places with help from friendly people who live in the area.

By choosing when and where to attack, a small band of guerrillas can make trouble for a far larger enemy force. Thousands of troops may fail to discover a handful of guerrillas if these can hide in a forest, a mountain range or a large city.

Guerrillas have fought in many wars this century in Europe, Africa, Asia and Central America.

**Mercenaries are soldiers prepared to fight in any war for any side that pays them. The word *mercenary* comes from a Latin word meaning 'wages'. Some fight just for money, others more for adventure.**

More than two thousand years ago, hired soldiers fought for the Persians, Greeks and Romans. About seven hundred years ago the warring kings and princes of Europe hired German and Swiss mercenaries. The mercenary Swiss Guard still protects the Vatican in Rome.

The most famous mercenary fighting unit has long been France's Foreign Legion. Its officers are almost all French, but many of its legionnaires are volunteers from other countries. Some are wanted criminals. The Legion takes anyone young and fit enough to fight unless it knows he is a murderer. Since 1960 some European mercenaries have fought in several African wars.

## ▲ WHAT IS A FRESCO?

**Frescoes are water-colour paintings made on a fresh, wet plaster surface. The word *fresco* is Italian for 'fresh'. Many frescoes are large paintings done on church walls.**

Making a fresco is quite complicated. First the artist makes a small coloured sketch of the picture. Next, he or she makes a full-size drawing called a cartoon. The artist takes a tracing of this and traces it on to a wall covered with wet plaster. Then he or she paints on the plaster before it dries. Fresco scenes have clear, pure colours.

The finest frescoes were painted in Renaissance Italy by artists such as Michelangelo, Raphael and Fra Angelico. The picture shows part of a fresco by Fra Angelico.

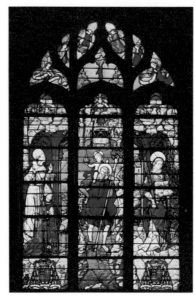

## ▲ WHAT IS STAINED GLASS?

**Stained glass is coloured glass used in windows. Pieces of differently coloured stained glass are fitted together in a frame to make a picture. Many churches have stained-glass windows.**

An artist first makes a coloured sketch of the window, showing the shapes, sizes and colours of its pieces of glass. The glass itself is coloured by chemicals while being made.

Workmen cut the glass into pieces to match those shown on the artist's full-scale drawing. Then the artist paints designs on the glass in coloured enamels. These are baked into the glass in a furnace. Lastly, the pieces of glass are fitted together with strips of lead.

## ▼ WHAT IS THE VENUS DE MILO?

**This famous Greek statue shows a beautiful woman representing the love goddess Venus (Aphrodite). It is called *de Milo* ('of Milos') because it was found on the Greek island of Milos.**

The statue was carved out of marble more than 2000 years ago, perhaps by the sculptor Agesandros of Alexandria. It was made in a style that was old even then.

For centuries the statue lay hidden in a cave. It was found in 1820, and was by then badly broken. Later, some of the pieces were lost, and now the statue lacks arms.

A French ambassador bought the Venus de Milo for King Louis XVIII. Today it is one of the great treasures of the Louvre Museum in Paris.

### ▼ WHAT IS IMPRESSIONISM?

**This is a style of painting that gives an impression of something, not an exact picture of it. It was first used by some French artists in the 1870s. They used dabs of pure colours to show objects as they appear in natural light.**

Impressionists did not try to paint details as exactly as most artists did. Instead they used blobs and strokes to try to catch the effects of light on a scene.

Unlike most artists, they did not like painting in a studio. They preferred to paint outdoors in natural light. Sometimes they painted the same scene several times as the light on it changed throughout the day.

The name Impressionism came from Claude Monet's painting *Impression: Sunrise*, which was shown at the first Impressionist exhibition held in 1874. Part of this picture is shown here. Other Impressionists included Camille Pissarro and Alfred Sisley.

### ▼ WHAT IS A LITHOGRAPH?

**Lithographs are copies of pictures produced by a printing process based on the fact that oil and water do not mix.**

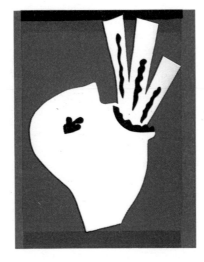

To make a lithograph, an artist uses a flat stone of a kind that will soak up oil and water. He or she draws a design on the stone with a greasy crayon. Then the artist dampens the stone with water. This soaks in only where no crayon marks cover the stone.

Next, the artist rolls oily printing ink over the stone's flat surface. The ink sticks only to the crayon, for water repels it.

The artist waits for the water to dry off. Then a sheet of paper is pressed onto the stone. The oily ink transfers a copy of the artist's design to the paper. Besides drawing in crayon, artists may draw or paint their designs in greasy ink.

The lithograph shown above, called *The Sword Swallower*, is by the French artist Henri Matisse.

### ▼ WHAT IS SURREALISM?

**This is art that tries to show things hidden deep in people's minds, or just strange, disturbing ideas and objects.**

Surrealism was begun in the 1920s by the French writer André Breton. But famous Surrealists have included Spanish painters such as Salvador Dali, and the Belgian painter René Magritte.

Dali painted lifelike objects arranged in impossible ways as if in some kind of dream. One picture of this kind shows watches as floppy as omelettes, draped over a strange countryside. Magritte painted unbelievable things like a boot with five toes. The painting shown here is by the German Surrealist Max Ernst.

There are also Surrealist sculptures. Spain's Joan Miró made one from a stuffed parrot, an artificial leg and a bowler hat. One of Dali's sculptures had snails crawling over a woman. Another sculptor produced a cup lined with fur! There are also Surrealist films and literature.

### ▶ WHAT IS A MIME?

**A mime is a silent play, or acting without words. Actors show what they mean by gestures and facial expressions instead of spoken words. Actors who work like this are also called mimes.**

In ancient Greece and Rome mimes were comic plays about absurd characters like stupid old men or ridiculous slaves.

Much later, actors played similar parts in Italian comedies of the kind called *commedia dell' arte*. The actors spoke, but also mimed emotions. Italian characters such as Harlequin found their way into English pantomime where at first all acting was mimed.

Modern mime acting began in the 1800s in France. The first great French mime was Jean-Baptiste-Gaspard Deburau, who died in 1846. Today, famous mimes such as Marcel Marceau imitate actions such as climbing stairs, cleaning windows or chasing a butterfly.

### ◀ WHAT IS A MYSTERY PLAY?

**Mystery plays were plays about Bible stories or saints' lives. They were performed outdoors in the Middle Ages.**

'Mystery' comes from the Latin word *ministerium*, meaning 'religious service'. The first mystery plays were acted by priests at services in churches.

Later, tradesmen, craftsmen and other groups put on plays outside churches.

In England, each trade or craft put on an appropriate play. For instance shipwrights, sailors and fishermen acted the story of Noah's Ark. Some mystery plays were acted on platforms. Others took place on wagons drawn through the streets.

A group of plays would be performed at festivals such as Easter or Christmas. Between them, the plays told all the important Bible stories. They taught people religious ideas in a lively, enjoyable way.

### ▶ WHAT IS KABUKI?

***Kabuki* is the name for a type of play performed in Japan. Its name means 'the art of singing and dancing'. Kabuki plays contain plenty of both.**

Many kabuki plays are about a string of exciting events, some of them magical. Actors wear elaborate costumes and their faces are heavily painted. Heroes are white but villains are reddish.

The actors, all men, often fight pretended duels, and mime actions such as drinking tea from invisible cups. Music is played all through each drama and the actors sing, rather like opera singers.

Each kabuki stage is wide, with runways that jut out into the audience. Much of the scenery is very solid and there are excitingly realistic stage effects. These may include, for instance, a village on fire.

A property man dressed in black moves scenery about on the stage during the play, but no one takes any notice of him.

### ▲ WHAT IS A FLYING BUTTRESS?

**A flying buttress is a special kind of side-support helping to hold up a tall building with an arched roof. Many Gothic churches have flying buttresses.**

Each flying buttress consists of a bar, an arch, or half an arch, that juts out from the upper part of a wall or pillar. This holds up an arched roof called a vault. The vault puts an outward strain on the wall or pillar. The flying buttress is supported by a buttress forming a solid stone or brick wall. This juts out sideways from the building's main wall, or a supporting pillar. Together, the flying buttress and buttress take the strain of the vault.

Pinnacles on top of the buttresses give them more weight, helping them resist the thrust from the side.

As church architects began to use flying buttresses, they could build high churches with slim walls instead of very much thicker walls.

### ◄ WHAT IS GOTHIC ARCHITECTURE?

**Gothic architecture is a style of building. It was used for many churches and some other buildings raised in Europe from about AD 1140 to 1500.**

A church built in the Gothic style tends to be very tall with pointed arches for the roof and windows. The main roof is supported by arched ribs held up by pillars, not by solid walls.

Between the pillars, tall stained-glass windows largely take the place of walls. Flying buttresses rest on stone supports outside the church and help to hold up its roof. Building in this style saved stone and made the inside of a church light and airy.

Many churches have a spire soaring high above the roof. Inside and out there may be carved stone figures of holy people mentioned in the Bible.

Critics who disliked the Gothic style named it after the Goths. These were uncivilized tribes who once invaded Roman Italy.

### ◄ WHAT IS ART NOUVEAU?

***Art nouveau* means 'new art'. It was a new style of art and architecture that started in Europe in the 1880s and spread to America.**

Many art nouveau artists and architects used designs with lines that curved like the stems of plants, flickering flames, or curling waves.

The English artist Aubrey Beardsley made delicate black-and-white ink drawings. Scotland's Charles Rennie Mackintosh designed sturdy furniture with simple shapes.

The Spanish architect Antoni Gaudí gave weird snaky shapes to the outsides of buildings. Victor Horta of Belgium designed a strange, writhing stairway and the stained-glass doors shown here.

Émile Gallé in France, Karl Koepping, in Germany, and Louis Tiffany, in the United States, made glass vases and other objects with delicate shapes and beautiful colours.

## ▶ WHAT IS A PENTATHLON?

**A pentathlon is a five-part competition for athletes. Its name comes from the Greek words *pente*, meaning five, and *athlon*, meaning contest. In a pentathlon each contestant must take part in five different events. The winner is the one with the highest score.**

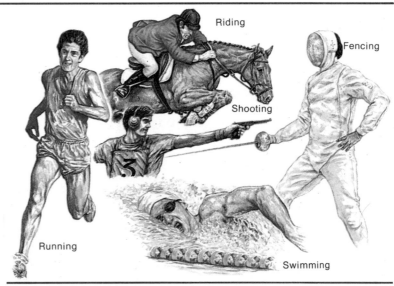

Riding

Fencing

Shooting

Running

Swimming

In ancient Greece and Rome the chosen events were ones thought to test all the strengths and skills of an athlete. These events were wrestling, foot racing, jumping, throwing the javelin and throwing the discus. The javelin was a light spear and the discus was a flat plate made of stone or metal. The athletes had to compete in all events in one day.

In 1912 the old Greek-style pentathlon was brought into the modern Olympic Games. But instead of wrestling, men ran a 1500-metre race.

At the same time, the Olympic Games started the brand-new modern or military pentathlon. This tests the abilities a messenger might have needed in the days of cavalry warfare. Its five events are riding, fencing, swimming, shooting and running 4000 metres.

The Olympic Games dropped the Greek-style pentathlon for men in 1924. In 1964 the Games brought in the women's pentathlon. Athletes competed in a high jump, long jump, 200-metre race, 80-metre race over hurdles, and the shot-put (throwing a heavy metal ball).

Later, women raced over 800 metres instead of 80, and over 100 metres of hurdles.

## ▼ WHAT IS THE WORLD SERIES?

**This is a series of baseball games held in the United States each October. It decides the top baseball team.**

The two rival teams are the year's champions of the top two American baseball leagues, the National League and the American League.

As in all baseball games, each team has nine players and most action happens on a diamond-shaped infield with a base at each corner. A pitcher throws a ball to a batter who tries to hit it and run to a base before he is made out by a fielder. A batter who safely reaches all bases scores a run.

A team's innings (turn to bat) ends when three batters are put out. Each game is won by the team scoring the most runs in nine innings.

In the World Series, the teams play the best of seven games. The winners are the first team to win four. Winners of the World Series become world champions.

### ▼ WHAT IS FIGURE SKATING?

**This is one of the three main ice-skating sports. (The other two are speed skating and ice dancing.) Figure skating involves skating patterns called figures on ice.**

Figure-skating contests have two main parts. These are school figures and free skating. School figures are based on a figure-of-eight

pattern, and may be skated on both skates or only one. They include about 70 variations. Skaters must try to make both circles of a figure-of-eight the same size, and there are rules for how to hold the body.

Free skating is freer than school figures. Skaters can leap, spin and make other smoothly-linked movements.

In pairs skating, a man and woman skate together. The man sometimes lifts the woman high in the air. For figure skating, skaters need specially shaped skates fixed to high, laced boots that fit very snugly.

### ▼ WHAT IS FORMULA ONE MOTOR RACING?

**This is the world's top-rank type of motor racing. All the most important of the Grand Prix races are those between Formula One racing cars.**

A Formula One racing car is low and wedge-shaped. The driver lies in a cockpit in front of the engine. This has a capacity of no more than 3 litres, or 1.5 litres if turbo-

charged or super-charged. It may not have more than 12 cylinders. The five- or six-speed gearbox lets the driver get the most power possible, whatever the speed of the car.

The car runs on broad, treadless tyres. These keep their grip with help from a wing-like aerofoil jutting up behind the engine.

Formula One cars can reach 320 kilometres an hour. The races are about 320 kilometres long. They are run on circuits with straight, fast stretches, and bends where drivers must brake and accelerate hard.

### ▼ WHAT IS THE FASTEST BALL GAME?

**This is one of several games played with a small, hard ball known as a *pelota* (the Spanish for ball). The fastest pelota game is known in Spanish as *pelota vasca*, meaning 'Basque pelota'. Its Basque name is *jaï alaï* or 'merry festival'. Jaï alaï may have begun in thirteenth-century Italy.**

Jaï alaï players wear a long, basket-like *cesta* strapped to one arm. They use the cesta's curved hollow end to catch and throw the small, hard rubber ball called a pelota. There are two rival teams, each with one, two or three players.

They play on a *cancha*, or court, with high walls on three sides. A server hits the ball on the front wall. Opponents must catch it and throw it back before it hits the floor twice.

The ball moves tremendously fast. One pelota reached a measured speed of over 300 kilometres an hour.

# INDEX

## PHOTOGRAPHIC ACKNOWLEDGEMENTS

Pages: 25 top right Bruce Coleman/Peter Davey, 51 J. Allan
Cash, 53 The Order of St. John, 60 Photo Library International,
67 Bicc Ltd, 68 top right DeBeers Ltd, 71 bottom Nasa, 72
bottom Zefa UK Ltd, 77 top California Institute of Technology
and Carnegie Institute of Washington, 80 middle Royal
Observatory, Edinburgh, 81 middle Royal Astronomical
Society, 86 Picturepoint, 89 top Victoria & Albert Museum,
London, 89 bottom Heather Angel, 91 Colin Crane/Met. Office,
92 Photri, USA, 93 top J. Allan Cash, 95 top Nature
Photographers/JV & GR Harrison, 96 Zefa UK Ltd, 101 top
right Zefa UK Ltd, 102 British Museum, 104 Illustrated London
News, 105 Zefa UK Ltd, 106 bottom Janet & Colin Bord, 107
middle left Fortean Picture Library, 108 top & middle Zefa UK
Ltd, 111 middle Mansell Collection, 111 bottom Picturepoint,
113 top right Frank Spooner Pictures, 114 top left Scala, Milan,
114 top right Sonia Halliday, 115 bottom left Scala, Milan, 115
top left E. T. Archive/Victoria & Albert Museum, 115 top right
Tate Gallery, London, 117 bottom Richard Bryant, 118 Frank
Spooner Pictures, 119 left & middle Colorsport.

Picture Research: Penny J. Warn.